LEGO

New sets based on movie scenes and vehicles for you to build and combine to make your own.

- Lightsabre Duel — £5.99
- Droid Starfighter — £5.99
- Naboo Swamp Diorama — £7.99
- Anakin's Podracer — £10.99
- Naboo Starfighter — £16.99
- Sith Infiltrator — £26.99
- Gungan Sub — £39.99
- Mos Espa Podrace Diorama — £69.99

Naboo Starfighter

Anakin's Podracer

Gungan Sub

Droid Starfighter

Sith Infiltrator

- **Room Alarm Destroyer Droid** — £35.99
  Motion activated room alarm with sounds from the movie. A great gift.

GRAPHIC NOVELS
- **Star Wars: Episode I – The Phantom Menace** – H Gilroy, R Damaggio, A Williamson — £9.99

MODEL KITS
A range of exciting and colourful model kits based on vehicles from the new movie. Please note, some kits may require some experience at model-making.

Droid Fighter

- Snapfast Naboo Starfighter — £9.99
- Snapfast Trade Federation Droid Fighter — £9.99
- Anakin's Podracer — £14.99
- Die-cast Naboo Starfighter — £19.99

Mini Model Kits — @£4.99
Small model versions of vehicles in the film.

- **Republic Cruiser**
- **Sith Spacecraft**
- **Trade Federation Landing Ship**
- **Trade Federation Large Transport**

MONEY BANKS
Interactive money banks featuring three characters from the film. When placed together, the electronic battle actions work together to recreate one of the key action sequences in the film.

- **Darth Maul** — £59.99
- **Qui-Gon Jinn** (July) — £59.99
- **Obi-Wan Kenobi** (August) — £59.99
Quality, 'slot-type' money banks — @£14.99
- **Jar Jar Binks**   • **Darth Maul**

ORGANISERS
- **Darth Maul Organiser** — £9.99
  Black vinyl with velcro fastener and Darth Maul on front panel.
- **Jar Jar Binks Organiser** — £12.99
  Blue vinyl with snap fastener and Jar Jar Binks on front panel.
- **Queen Amidala Organiser** — £12.99
  Red, 'velvet' finish vinyl with snap fastener and Queen Amidala on front panel.
- **Lightsabre Logo** — £15.99
  Black canvas with zip fastener and Episode I Lightsabre logo on front panel.

POSTERS — @£6.99
Genuine replica movie posters. (136cm x 96cm)
- **One-sheet** (*The* movie poster)
- **Teaser** (Anakin with Darth Vader shadow)

ROLE-PLAY
- **Foam Projectile Blaster** — £9.99
  Modelled on the Naboo blaster featured in the film. Fires harmless foam projectiles.
- **Role-Play Blaster** — £14.95
  Electronic Tatooine blaster pistol modelled on the ones used in the movie.
- **Jedi Role-Play Set** — £22.99
  Practice your Jedi skills with this great play set. Includes belt, comm reader and lightsabre as featured in the film.
- **Jedi Lightsabre** — £24.99
  Replica of the lightsabre used by Obi-Wan Kenobi and Qui-Gon Jinn.
- **Sith Double Lightsabre** — £39.99
  A copy of the double lightsabre used by the evil Sith Lord, Darth Maul.

WALL PLANNERS — @£9.99
Double-sided wall planners with scenes and characters from the film. Academic year Jul 1999 to Jun 2000 on one side and calendar year Jan-Dec 2000 on the reverse.
- **Queen Amidala**   • **Space Battle**

- **Podr ace**
- **Darth Maul**
- **Obi-Wan Kenobi**
- **Jar Jar Binks**

WIPE-ON/ WIPE-OFF BOARDS — @£14.99
Academic Calendar (Jul 1999 to Jun 2000), flexible wipe-on/wipe-off boards for writing messages, notes, birthdays and reminders. Each design is available in die-cut or magnetic versions.
- **Jar Jar Binks**   • **Darth Maul**
- **R2-D2**   • **Yoda**

TIES
- **SILK** — @£14.99
- **POLYESTER** — @£9.99
Quality silk and polyester ties featuring characters, scenes and designs from the new film.
- **Battle Droids**   • **Jedi Logo** (Blue)
- **R2-D2**   • **Darth Maul Tattoo**
Ties available only in polyester.
- **Darth Maul Poses**
- **'Eyes of Maul'**   • **Sith Lord**
- **Jar Jar Binks**   • **Naboo**

STAR WARS

STAR WARS
EPISODE I

Collect it.

Trade it.

Play it.

Use the Force...

Anywhere.

With the Young Jedi Collectible Card Game, you can carry the magic of *Star Wars* in your back pocket.

The first expansion of the Young Jedi Collectible Card Game, titled Menace of Darth Maul, released in May 1999 and contains 140 game cards plus the special set of 18 super rare foil cards. Cards are distributed in starter decks of 60 and booster packs of 11. Starter decks are pre-constructed and contain 10 cards not found in the booster packs. Foil cards appear only in the booster packs.

Two further expansions will be released in 1999, bringing the total number of cards to well over 400!

Visit www.decipher.com for further information.

DECIPHER®
The Art of Great Games®

STAR WARS
EPISODE I
THE PHANTOM MENACE

Published in association with the Topps Company, Inc.

Original Editor
Bob Woods

Design
Mada Design, Inc.

Contributing Writers
Marc Patten
Mark Cotta Vaz

Special thanks to
Linda Baker, Len Brown
Cara Evangelista, Ira Friedman,
Gary Gerani, Lynne Hale Josh Izzo, Stacy Mollema
Matt Olsen, Ellen Pasternack,
Howard Roffman,
Scott Silverstein
John Williams, Tim Wills Nagisa Yamamoto

Lucas Licensing
Director of Publishing
Lucy Autrey Wilson

Continuity Editor
Allan Kausch

EVERY SAGA HAS A BEGINNING

Star Wars has become an uncommonly strong, powerful and positive influence on our culture. Who hasn't heard of Luke Skywalker, Darth Vader, R2-D2 and C-3PO? Yoda has emerged as a modern-day philosopher, and being with the Force is a well-wishing desired everywhere. More than a highly entertaining movie that first swept up hero-hungry audiences in 1977, Star Wars represents a uniquely potent movement that transcends the cinema. Combining its archetypical heroes and villains, its enchanting fantasy worlds and bizarre aliens, its marvelous starships and special effects, Star Wars is a myth for the ages.

For more than 20 years, the whole of Star Wars—which includes A New Hope's sequel parts, The Empire Strikes Back and Return of the Jedi— has endured as Episodes IV, V and VI. All along, however, we've known that its creator, George Lucas, harbors more about his multi-part saga and its tangled web of characters, that there is a "back story" to it all. Now, with Star Wars: Episode I The Phantom Menace, the first in a trilogy of long-awaited prequels, we're finally getting a glimpse.

We meet young Anakin Skywalker, the slave boy who grows up to become Darth Vader. We meet Obi-Wan Kenobi, who will train Anakin in the mysterious ways of the Jedi and later witness his agonizing defection to the dark side. We meet the droids R2-D2 and C-3PO and find out how their mechanical paths first cross. We discover how Palpatine stealthily orchestrates his rise to power. In the end, we gain a sense of the menace that awaits us in Episodes II and III.

This official publication is a keepsake companion to The Phantom Menace. Besides concisely retelling the story with vivid images directly from the movie, it delves into the entire making of the film—from the day Lucas began writing the script in 1996 to the months just prior to its May 19, 1999 release, when ILM was finishing up its gargantuan post-production task. See fascinating concept art, tour the "creature shop," learn how the costumes were designed. Go behind the scenes at England's Leavesden Studios, and travel to Italy and Tunisia for location shoots. Throughout the magazine, hear from the cast and crew about their incredible Episode I experiences.

The original Star Wars tale still affects people around the world in very personal ways, and now Episode I The Phantom Menace will launch a new journey into ageless storytelling. The film marks another milestone in moviemaking, and the story of how it all came together is right in your hands.

May the Force be with you... always.

Bob Woods, Editor

For Titan

Editor
Marcus Hearn

Senior Designer
Oz Browne

Managing Editor
John Freeman

Editorial Assistant
Martin Eden

Production Co-ordinator
Ben Gibbons

Production Controller
Bob Kelly

Circulation Co-ordinator
Rachael Kitts

LA Liaison
Lou Anders

Sales Consultant
David Orme

Marketing and Promotions Manager
Katherine Kleeb

Marketing & Media Sales Director
Scott Ferguson-Caisley

Art Director
Chris Teather

Operations Director
Leigh Baulch

Executive Director
Vivian Cheung

Publisher
Nick Landau

Advertising
Miles Dunbar
Tel: 0171 620 0200

Distribution
Comag
Tel: 01895 444055

Account Executive
Richard Kingerlee

Subscriptions
Tel: 01536 763631

STAR WARS

EPISODE I

THE PHANTOM MENACE

THE BLOCKADE

A long time ago in a galaxy far, far away… The powerful and sinister Trade Federation is threatening the stability of the Galactic Republic. To challenge the government's taxation of intergalactic trade routes, the Trade Federation has mustered a space blockade around the peaceful planet of Naboo. Hoping to quell the tense situation and fortify Naboo's newly elected Queen Amidala, the Supreme Chancellor of the Republic, Valorum, dispatches two Jedi ambassadors, Qui-Gon Jinn and his apprentice, Obi-Wan Kenobi.

▲ DARTH SIDIOUS, COMMUNICATING WITH NUTE GUNRAY AND RUNE HAAKO VIA HOLOGRAM, ORDERS THE ASSASSINATION OF THE TWO JEDI.

NAME:
NUTE GUNRAY
SPECIES:
NEIMOIDIAN
STATUS:
TRADE FEDERATION
VICEROY ASSIGNED BY
DARTH SIDIOUS TO
OVERSEE INVASION
OF NABOO

When they dock their vessel on the Trade Federation's command battleship, the Jedi are met by the Neimoidian Viceroy Nute Gunray and his lieutenant Rune Haako, who have more than friendly diplomacy in mind. They have been ordered, by Darth Sidious—an evil Sith Lord who reveals himself as the menacing force behind the blockade—to assassinate the Jedi and launch an armed invasion of Naboo.

The unsuspecting Jedi are ambushed by a poisonous gas and lethal droids . They must summon their Force powers, as well as their legendary lightsaber skills, to narrowly escape the attack. Yet this is only the beginning of a portentous adventure that will transform the galaxy.

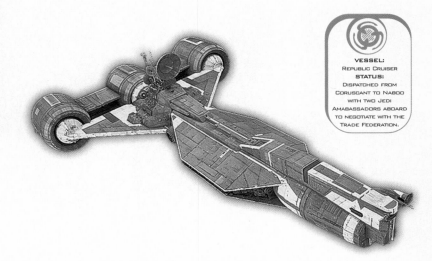

VESSEL:
REPUBLIC CRUISER
STATUS:
DISPATCHED FROM
CORUSCANT TO NABOO
WITH TWO JEDI
AMABASSADORS ABOARD
TO NEGOTIATE WITH THE
TRADE FEDERATION.

▲ AS THE REPUBLIC CRUISER BEARING QUI-GON AND OBI-WAN APPROACHES NABOO AND PASSES THROUGH THE TRADE FEDERATION BLOCKADE, THE JEDI HAVE NO IDEA OF THE DANGER AWAITING THEM.

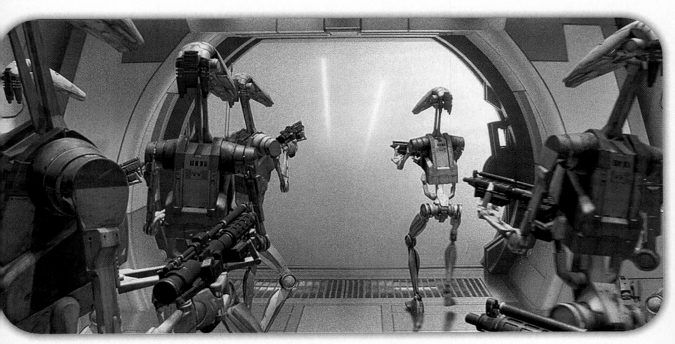

▲ NEITHER BATTLE DROIDS NOR POISON GAS, THOUGH, CAN OVERPOWER THEM.

THE INVASION BEGINS

Darth Sidious' nefarious plot unfolds as his minions deploy thousands of deadly battle droids and destroyer droids to the surface of Naboo. Qui-Gon and Obi-Wan, stowed away on two of the landing craft, witness the initiation of a massive invasion, soon realizing that the innocent planet's fate—indeed, that of the entire Republic—hangs in the balance.

VESSEL:
TRADE FEDERATION
TROOP TRANSPORT
STATUS:
FLOWN TO THE SURFACE
OF NABOO ABOARD
LANDING CRAFT, EACH
CARRIES HUNDREDS
OF DROIDS.

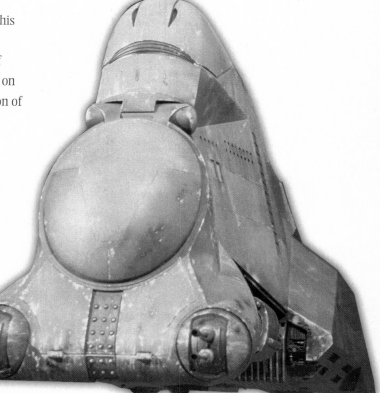

Carefully monitoring the dangerous events from a swampy hideout, the Jedi by chance meet an odd, amphibious creature, Jar Jar Binks. Jar Jar is a member of the indigenous Gungan species, which inhabits Naboo's underwater city, Otoh Gunga, and is separate and distrustful of the "outlanders" above.

NAME:
BATTLE DROID
STATUS:
TRADE FEDERATION LANDS
THOUSANDS OF DROIDS,
SOME WHICH RIDE STAP
VEHICLES, ON THE
SURFACE OF NABOO.

Meanwhile, Queen Amidala is adamant in defying the invading forces, yet the young monarch soon realizes that her volunteer security forces are no match for the Trade Federation's mighty mechanical troops and weaponry. She and her trusted aides—including Governor Sio Bibble, Captain Panaka and several handmaidens—concede that the situation is grave, but are unsure how to save Naboo.

UNDERSEA ADVENTUI

Qui-Gon convinces Jar Jar to guide him and Obi-Wan to Otoh Gunga, where the Jedi might better react to the impending invasion. The bungling Gungan leads them along an underwater route to the fantastic subterranean city, which exists inside a series of strange, bubble-like membranes.

Unfortunately, Jar Jar's reception by his fellow Gungans and their leader, Boss Nass, is anything but warm. It turns out that Jar Jar had been banished from Otoh Gunga, mostly for his careless, clumsy ways. Boss Nass rejects the Jedi's pleas for help against the invaders, though he agrees to spare Jar Jar's life and to provide the trio with a submarine that can take them through the planet's watery core and up to Theed, the outlanders' lush capital city, and Amidala's palace.

The journey aboard the squid-like "bongo" proves perilous. The vessel is attacked by one huge sea creature after another, each ready to devour the bongo and its defenseless passengers.

NAME: Boss Nass
SPECIES: Gungan
STATUS: The leader of the Gungans at first does not realize the threat posed by the Trade Federation's invasion of Naboo.

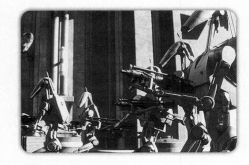

▲ THE JEDI AND JAR JAR'S JOURNEY FROM OTOH GUNGA TO THEED IN THE BONGO IS FRAUGHT WITH PERIL, AS THE SUBMARINE IS ATTACKED BY GIANT SEA MONSTERS.

◀ THEIR SUBSEQUENT PLAN TO FLEE NABOO WITH AMIDALA IS NO LESS FOREBODING, WITH BATTLE DROIDS INTENT ON THWARTING THEM THIS TIME.

Darth Sidious, fearing a hitch in his dastardly plot, orders his Viceroy to capture the Queen. Luckily, Qui-Gon and Obi-Wan rescue Amidala and convince her that their best chance to turn back the Trade Federation is to personally plead Naboo's case before the Republic Senate in Coruscant. The departure, though, isn't easy. They must battle their way through a battalion of droids before escaping in the Queen's Royal Starship.

VESSEL: Queen Amidala's Royal Starship
STATUS: With the Jedi, the Queen and her entourage aboard, it narrowly escapes Naboo enroute to Coruscant.

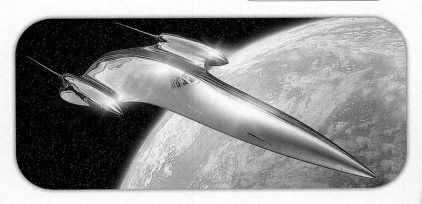

REPAIR TO TATOOINE

The flight though Naboo's blockaded airspace is no joyride. The Queen's transport, defenseless but for deflector shields, is buffeted by the Trade Federation battleship, and if not for a resourceful astromech droid aboard—later identified as R2-D2—it might have been destroyed. However, the ship's hyperdrive is too badly damaged to make it as far as Coruscant, so the crew decides to reroute to Tatooine, a rogue planet controlled by the Hutts, for repairs.

Qui-Gon, Artoo, Jar Jar and Padmé Naberrie, the Queen's most-trusted handmaiden, venture into Mos Espa in search of a hyperdrive generator. They encounter a shifty junk dealer, Watto, with whom Qui-Gon attempts to bargain for the part. Yet not even Jedi mind tricks can convince the wily Toydarian to accept Republic credits as payment. More fortuitously, they meet Watto's slave boy, Anakin Skywalker, who strikes up an immediate friendship with the travelers.

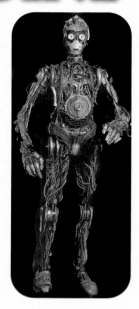

NAME: C-3PO
STATUS: PROTOCOL DROID BUILT BY ANAKIN FOR HIS MOTHER, SHMI SKYWALKER, FROM SPARE PARTS

NAME: R2-D2
STATUS: ASTROMECH DROID DISTINGUISHES ITSELF BY REPAIRING THE SHIELDS ON THE QUEEN'S DAMAGED STARSHIP

QUI-GON, JAR JAR AND PADMÉ EXPLORE THE STREETS OF MOS ESPA IN SEARCH OF A HYPERDRIVE GENERATOR FOR THE QUEEN'S SHIP.
▼

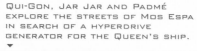

NAME:
WATTO
SPECIES:
TOYDARIAN
STATUS:
MOS ESPA JUNK DEALER
ACQUIRED SLAVES ANAKIN
AND SHMI SKYWALKER IN
A PODRACE BET

Together, they walk the busy streets of Mos Espa, trying to figure a way out of their plight. Jar Jar's high-jinks nearly land him in trouble with an alien tough named Sebulba, until Anakin intercedes. Meantime, a blinding sandstorm is kicking up, and the boy invites his new friends to wait it out at his house. There, he introduces them to his mother, Shmi (also a slave owned by Watto), and the protocol droid he's building, C-3PO. Qui-Gon grows intrigued with Anakin, not only for his mechanical prowess but also because of the special powers he senses.

The Jedi is further fascinated by Anakin's tales of Podracing, a reckless sport in which he navigates a small cockpit, tethered to gigantic, powerful engines, along a treacherous desert course. When Qui-Gon learns that Anakin has built his own Podracer, he begins mulling over an interesting solution to their dilemma.

THE PODRACE

The Boonta Eve Classic is the biggest Podrace of the year. The arena is sold out, filled to capacity with more than 100,000 rabid fans, who've come to cheer for—and bet on—their favorite pilots. No wager has more at stake, though, than the one Qui-Gon proposes to Watto. If Anakin—young as he is, the only human driver capable of competing at this level—wins, not only does Qui-Gon get the new hyperdrive generator he needs to repair the Queen's starship and continue their mission to Coruscant, but Anakin gains his freedom.

Jabba the Hutt, Tatooine's unscrupulous crime lord, introduces the field of racers, and they're off! To no one's surprise, Sebulba, the superstar of the Podracing circuit, takes the early lead and appears in control as the furious, thrill-a-second race unfolds. Anakin, who appeared doomed when his rig stalls, uses his keen piloting skills and strong will to pull even with Sebulba on the final lap. Despite the Dug's cutthroat efforts, Anakin prevails and wins.

NAME: Sebulba
SPECIES: Dug
STATUS: Renowned as much for his keen Podracing skills as he is for the unscrupulous maneuvers he pulls; uses his feet to operate his racer

NAME: Darth Maul
SPECIES: Humanoid
STATUS: Apprentice to the Sith Lord Darth Sidious is sent to disrupt the mission of Queen Amidala and the Jedi

▲ THE THRILL OF ANAKIN'S WIN IN THE PODRACE IS OFFSET WHEN HE GAINS HIS FREEDOM BUT MUST LEAVE HIS MOTHER BEHIND.

THEN THEIR FLIGHT FROM TATOOINE IS NEARLY SPOILED BY DARTH MAUL, WHO AMBUSHES QUI-GON, SPARKING A VICIOUS LIGHTSABER DUEL. ▶

The victory is bittersweet, however, when it comes time for Anakin to bid a tearful farewell to his mother, who must remain in servitude to Watto. "I will become a Jedi," the boy promises Shmi, "and come back and free you, Mom... I promise."

With the ship's repairs complete, the group is prepared to depart Tatooine, when Qui-Gon is suddenly attacked by the Sith apprentice Darth Maul, who has been ordered by Darth Sidious to intercept the party. A fierce lightsaber duel ensues, during which Qui-Gon must summon all his Jedi powers. He narrowly escapes, thankful as the Royal Starship speeds toward Coruscant, though anxious about the nature of his vicious assailant.

FATEFUL MEETINGS

The Queen's starship arrives safely at the Republic capital, Coruscant, a dazzling metropolis and seat of the Galactic Senate, as well as the Jedi Council. While Amidala confers with Naboo's Senator Palpatine about how to deal with their planet's worsening plight—he suggests that she forestall political haggling by calling for a Senate vote of no-confidence in Supreme Chancellor Valorum—Qui-Gon and Obi-Wan report to the Jedi Council's 12 members.

▲ THE JEDI COUNCIL INTENTLY CONSIDERS WHETHER ANAKIN SHOULD BE TRAINED TO BECOME ONE OF THEM, BUT ULTIMATELY REJECTS QUI-GON'S PROPOSAL.

◀ PALPATINE CONVINCES AMIDALA TO HAVE HIS FELLOW SENATORS DETERMINE CHANCELLOR VALORUM'S FATE. WHEN IT LEADS TO A VOTE OF NO-CONFIDENCE, PALPATINE EMERGES AS THE HEIR APPARENT.

NAME: MACE WINDU
SPECIES: HUMAN
STATUS: A SENIOR MEMBER
OF JEDI COUNCIL, HE IS
WARY WHEN LEARNING THAT
THE SITH MAY STILL EXIST

The council is both mystified and deeply concerned to learn that the Sith, practitioners of the dark side thought to be long extinct, may still be lurking, and, worse yet, involved with the Trade Federation. Adding another piece to the evolving puzzle, Qui-Gon introduces Anakin to his fellow Jedi, suggesting that he be tested for what Qui-Gon suspects is an extraordinary aptitude for the Force. Indeed, the tests bear out Qui-Gon's case for training Anakin to become a Jedi, but the council refuses, saying the boy is too old and possesses too much fear and anger.

The Queen is similarly frustrated as she implores the Senate to intervene in Naboo's dire situation. Finally, she agrees to Palpatine's proposal. After the no-confidence vote in Valorum passes, neither she nor the government officials suspect anything sinister when Palpatine is nominated to succeed Valorum as Supreme Chancellor of the Republic.

THE STORY

A CALL TO ARMS

THE HEROES RETURN TO NABOO, INTENT ON DEFENDING THE PEACEFUL PLANET FROM THE INVADING FORCES. ▶

YET THE ONLY WAY TO SAVE NABOO IS TO ENLIST THE HELP OF BOSS NASS AND THE GUNGAN ARMY. ▼

Queen Amidala, aware that the fate of Naboo is growing dimmer by the hour, elects to return home. Qui-Gon and Obi-Wan are instructed by the Jedi Council to accompany and protect her—and to find out more of the Sith threat. Take Anakin, too, they are told, but do not train him in the ways of the Jedi.

◀ DARTH MAUL MAY
HAVE FAILED TO STOP
THE QUEEN'S PARTY
ON TATOOINE, BUT HE
FOLLOWS THEM TO
NABOO, DETERMINED
TO FULFILL HIS
MASTER SIDIOUS'
DEADLY BIDDING.

Darth Sidious resolves not to let them upset his wicked conspiracy. He orders Nute Gunray to eliminate the Queen upon her arrival back on Naboo, while Darth Maul is sent there to destroy the Jedi.

During the flight home, Jar Jar assures the Queen that the Gungans are great warriors, capable of turning back the Trade Federation invaders. Amidala then becomes convinced that the only way to liberate Naboo is for her people to join the Gungans in a war against the Trade Federation's insurgents. That is precisely the plan proposed to Boss Nass, who has led the citizens of Otoh Gunga into hiding in the swamps. Initially, he balks at the notion—until Padmé reveals herself as the actual Queen, disguised as a handmaiden before now for security purposes. Boss Nass is touched by Amidala's impassioned plea for unity among all the people of Naboo, and pledges that the Gungans will fight to preserve their planet.

BATTLE OF NABOO

The portentous battle of Naboo begins on the planet's grassy plains. The Gungan armies, determined to defend their homeland, have mounted shield generators on massive fambaa beasts to deflect the artillery blasts of the Trade Federation's droid forces. They draw the masses of battle droids away from Theed so that the second part of the plan can be executed.

At Theed, a fleet of sleek Naboo fighters, led by the veteran pilot Ric Olié, is dispatched to target the Trade Federation battleship carrying the device that controls the droids on the ground. By destroying that ship, and simultaneously overpowering Nute Gunray and his minions commanding the invasion from Theed, Naboo might still be saved. No one notices, however, as the fighters blast off from the besieged hangar, that Anakin and R2-D2 have taken refuge in one.

▲ THE ENDLESS CHARGE OF BATTLE
DROIDS, PLUS THE MIGHT OF THE TRADE
FEDERATION'S TANK TROOPS, PRESENT A
MAJOR CHALLENGE TO THE GUNGAN ARMY.

◄ WILL QUI-GON AND OBI-WAN FARE BETTER
AGAINST THE POWERFUL DARTH MAUL?

As the frenzied space battle ensues,
back at the palace Darth Maul enters the
fray, engaging Qui-Gon and Obi-Wan in
a brutal lightsaber fight. Deftly wielding
his double-bladed saber, the powerful
Sith is a formidable opponent, even for
two skilled Jedi.

ANAKIN SAVES THE DAY

■The fleet of Naboo fighters appears unable to penetrate the Trade Federation battleship—until the one piloted by Anakin breaks through and fires the decisive shot.

The Trade Federation appears to be winning the space battle, too, as the valiant Naboo fighters are no match for the endless swarms of droid spacecraft. But, wait, there is a lone Naboo ship—the one occupied by Anakin and that has been inadvertently launched into the conflict—that may yet complete the mission. Desperately dodging enemy fire, Anakin crash-lands his fighter inside the targeted Trade Federation battleship. Just before Anakin's stalled craft can be captured by battle droids, it lifts off, and Anakin fires two torpedoes that are headed straight for the critical power generators.

Kaboom! They hit their mark, and just as the giant vessel blows apart, Anakin and Artoo escape unscathed. Simultaneously, the droids on the ground are rendered powerless, literally stalling in their tracks, allowing the Gungan warriors to seize control. And when Amidala's troops overpower the Viceroy Nute Gunray, the Trade Federation's vile scheme is effectively squashed.

There is one pivotal battle still being waged, however: the furious lightsaber fight between Darth Maul and Qui-Gon and Obi-Wan. Indeed, when the Jedi become separated by a deadly laser wall, Obi-Wan helplessly watches as his mentor is cut down. Darth Maul proves no match for the inspired young Jedi; Obi-Wan strikes the final blow as Maul plunges to his death into the power generator pit.

THE STORY

PEACE PREVAILS... FOR NOW

Order has been restored to the galaxy. The Trade Federation's invading forces have been defeated and driven from Naboo. Palpatine has begun his stealthily orchestrated regime as the Republic's newly elected Supreme Chancellor. Obi-Wan, deeply saddened by the loss of Qui-Gon, is now a full-fledged Jedi and has been granted permission—if reluctantly—to take Anakin as his apprentice. To celebrate the mutual victory over their oppressors, all the people of Naboo, including the Gungans, come together for a triumphant parade in the central plaza of Theed.

There is one unresolved matter, though, that leaves the Jedi Council with a grave uneasiness. As Yoda and Mace Windu realize, with the Sith, there are always two, a master and an apprentice. They know that one has been destroyed. Is it the master or the apprentice…?

THE SERVANT

THE MOST SOPHISTICATED STAR W

OF THE FORCE MUST PREVAIL...

QUI-GON JINN

Qui-Gon is a consummate, if sometimes renegade Jedi Master, wise in the ways of nature and the Force. Even as he kindles that knowledge in his apprentice, Obi-Wan Kenobi, Qui-Gon seeks the Jedi Council's permission to also train Anakin.

LIAM NEESON

If you've ever had the impression that Neeson, a native son of Ballymena, Northern Ireland, was about to box someone's ears off, there's a good reason for it. As a young lad, Neeson was a boxing champ before turning his rather large hands to forklift operating, truck driving and a stint as an assistant architect. Then acting came calling, and Neeson answered the bell. The impetus to his thespian career was an advertisement posted by the Lyric Players' Theater in Belfast stating the need for a tall man to perform a bit part. Neeson fit the bill perfectly and ended up staying with the company for two years before being discovered by director John Boorman, who cast him as Sir Gawain in 1981's *Excalibur*. He moved on to play a variety of film roles, perhaps most notably as the dark hero of *Darkman*, before fame scored a technical knockout over the actor when he was cast as the title character in Steven Spielberg's *Schindler's List*. Neeson also appeared in the role of Jean Valjean in the screen adaptation of Victor Hugo's *Les Miserables* and in the title role in Neil Jordan's *Michael Collins*. As for his part in *The Phantom Menace*, Neeson says he was drawn to the role because "it's wonderful to play heroes. I feel we don't have enough of them. The character I play in *Star Wars* is as close as you can get to an old-time kind of warrior-sage, who is wise and who has supreme confidence, who yet has a kind of magical ability to see into the future."

OBI-WAN KENOBI

Qui-Gon's apprentice finds ample opportunity to hone his Jedi skills while at his mentor's side. He proves himself worthy on several occasions, enough so that he is entrusted to train another initiate whose fate will affect the entire galaxy.

EWAN McGREGOR

Young Ewan McGregor got into acting because his uncle, Denis Lawson, was making money at it. Uncle Denis even had a role in *Star Wars*, playing Wedge in the original trilogy. McGregor left home to study acting at 16, first at the Perth Repertory Company, then at London's Guildhall School of Music and Drama. His first movie job was the role of Alvarez in Bill Forsyth's quirky 1993 film *Being Human*, with Robin Williams. The movie—and McGregor—were quickly forgotten. But in 1994, he met a director-producer-writer trio who would really launch his career. Danny Boyle, Andrew MacDonald and John Hodge cast him in *Shallow Grave*, a macabre thriller that became a big hit. The same group got back together for *Trainspotting*, another enormous success in Britain and abroad. McGregor also appeared in *Emma* with Gwyneth Paltrow, Petar Greenaway's *The Pillow Book* and *Brassed Off* before the *Trainspotting* team reunited a third time for *A Life Less Ordinary*, their first American film. Since then he has appeared in *Velvet Goldmine* and *Little Voice*. But he still remembers *Star Wars* movies from a long time ago. "They were completely engrossing," he says. "When you watch them as a child, they take over. I used to play *Star Wars* all the time." And when he was called to play young Obi-Wan Kenobi, he says, "You can't say no, can you, if they ask you to do it? It's to be part of a legend, part of a modern myth. And to see yourself in space, that's kind of cool."

ANAKIN SKYWALKER

Living with his mother in servitude to Watto, young Anakin is renowned in Mos Espa for his uncanny Podracing skills. Yet when Amidala's Royal Starship makes an unscheduled stop on Tatooine and Anakin encounters her entourage, Qui-Gon foresees a far greater destiny for the boy.

JAKE LLOYD

Lloyd may have just turned 10, but after only a few short years in the business, he has a résumé that would make any actor proud. He landed his first feature film, *Unhook the Stars*, when he was just six years old. Lloyd then went on to star with his hero, Arnold Schwarzenegger, in *Jingle All the Way*. He has guest starred on such hit TV shows as *ER* and *The Pretender*. He enjoyed playing young Angelo, an autistic character on *The Pretender*, because it challenged him to find new and creative ways to express what his character was feeling. When he first heard that he got the part of Anakin in Episode I, Lloyd says, "I started bawling, I was so happy." As to his feelings of playing such an evil character, he replies, "Darth Vader has always been my favorite character. He's not such a bad guy. After all, he killed the Emperor. Nobody else could do that!" Currently finishing 4th grade, Lloyd lives in Southern California with his parents and younger sister, Madison. When he's not working, he enjoys riding his bike, playing video games and spending time with his friends.

SHMI SKYWALKER

A mother's unconditional love for her son runs so deep in Shmi that she is willing to let Anakin leave home and follow his destiny with the Jedi, even though she must stay behind as Watto's slave in Mos Espa.

PERNILLA AUGUST

Swedish actress August most recently worked with the legendary Liv Ullman and Ingmar Bergman in *The Confession*, a film directed by Ullman and written by Bergman, who had previously directed August in *Fanny and Alexander*. In 1992, she won the Best Actress Award at the Cannes Film Festival for her performance in The Best Intentions, also written by Bergman. August's theater credits include *The Dream Play*, *Hamlet* (for which she won the British Drama Magazine's Best Supporting Actress Award playing Ophelia), *The Dolls House* and *The Winter's Tale*, all directed by Bergman and performed at the National Theater of Sweden. What she found to be the most difficult thing to do in *The Phantom Menace*, she says, "was to speak English in a movie. It's very hard to play in another language. I was very nervous about it. But George Lucas was so sweet the first time we met. I said, 'How about an accent? What should I do about it?' He said, 'Don't worry. She's coming from a Swedish galaxy.'"

THE CAST

QUEEN AMIDALA

PHOTO BY NIGEL PARRY CRD

Although she's only 14, Amidala wields tremendous power as the newly elected Queen of Naboo. She uses it wisely in defending her people from the Trade Federation's invading forces.

NATALIE PORTMAN

Portman's story about how she started her film career sounds like a Hollywood cliché. "I was in a pizza parlor after dance class one day when I was 11, and a man from Revlon saw me and wanted me to model," she says, recalling the 1992 encounter that changed her life. "I said I wanted to act, so he introduced me to an agent. I started going on auditions, and that was it." Her first role, as the young girl who befriends hitman Jean Reno in *The Professional*, was a tour de force performance from the then 12 year old. She has since appeared in *Everyone Says I Love You*, *Mars Attacks!*, *Heat*, *Beautiful Girls* and *Anywhere But Here*. Born in Jerusalem, Portman admits that growing up, she wasn't a huge *Star Wars* fan, but "my cousins were obsessed with it." Regarding Amidala, she says, "I hope she is a role model. It's good for girls to see an action hero who is like them, because usually you only see guys being action heroes. She is really strong and smart, and basically she leads her people to victory in the war. She saves all her people, which is cool for young girls to see."

JAR JAR BINKS

Banished from the underwater city of Otoh Gunga, mostly for his bumbling ways, Jar Jar is befriended by Qui-Gon and Obi-Wan during the invasion of Naboo. He accompanies them on their adventures, eventually returning home to fight alongside his fellow amphibious Gungans.

AHMED BEST

Best was just "stomping" around on stage when he got called into the *Star Wars* fold. Until then, his only other non-student film work had been in *Lean on Me*. He was performing in the percussion theater piece *Stomp* when *Star Wars* Casting Director Robin Gurland happened to catch the show and afterward started the ball rolling. Now it's come full circle for Best. "*Star Wars* was the first movie I ever saw," he says. "I was three years old when it came out. I vividly remember walking into the theater, sitting down and watching the entire movie. And I remember it just blowing my mind. I never forgot the whole *Star Wars* experience. It made me love movies. It made me want to get into performance, get into theater, get into acting. *Star Wars* is probably as big as it gets, as far as movies go. It can't help but change your life in some way. I mean, this is a piece of history."

USE THE FORCE
NEW

THERE'S A NEW DISTURBANCE IN THE FORCE... AND IT'S COMING FROM LEGO®.

BUILD AND PLAY THE PLOT OF THE NEW STAR WARS MOVIE. AND THEN USE YOUR IMAGINATION AND MAKE YOUR OWN STORY.

THE COMBINATION OF LEGO AND YOUR CREATIVITY IS UNBEATABLE - EVEN FOR DARTH MAUL.

STAR WARS™

LEGO®
just imagine...

COLLECT ALL THE LEGO STAR WARS SETS

GUNGAN™ SUB SITH INFILTRATOR™ NABOO FIGHTER™ MOS ESPA PODRACE™ DROID FIGHTER™

THE CAST

R2-D2

Seemingly just another astromech droid in the Queen's service, R2-D2's mettle is tested—and passes with flying colors—when Amidala's Royal Starship is attacked. That will not be the last time the endearing droid's heroics save the day.

KENNY BAKER

Kenny Baker has always used his diminutive size to his advantage. Born in Birmingham, England, Baker joined a stage show when he was just 16. Three years later, he attached himself to Billy Smart's circus as a ringmaster and clown before forming a comedy and musical team with another little person that traveled the world. When initially contacted to step "inside" the role of R2-D2, Baker turned down the part, because he thought it would be too uncomfortable inside what he called a "metal vacuum cleaner." But he finally agreed to give a human dimension to the three-legged R2-series astromech droid. Outside of Artoo and *Star Wars*, Baker has distinguished himself in such films as *The Elephant Man*, *Time Bandits* and *Amadeus*.

C-3PO

Anakin demonstrates his keen sense for mechanics by building a protocol droid from spare parts. The boy has no idea when he leaves home without C-3PO—yet in the company of another droid, R2-D2—what future events will bring all three of them together.

ANTHONY DANIELS

In 1976, Daniels had been seriously acting for only two years and was reluctant to accept the role of the character C-3PO, thinking it a mere machine. But after reading the script for the original *Star Wars*, he was convinced otherwise. His first appearance in the Tunisian desert as Threepio took the assistance of six dressers working more than two hours to get him ready. "Mind you," he says, "when I stepped out into the desert sun, I did have a moment of glory. Everyone reacted as if I was some sort of god." Daniels has been closely involved with the character ever since. Despite varied roles in theater and TV, he will always be indelibly linked with the quirky mannerisms and equally quirky voice of the lovable and sensitive droid. "I guess we've grown attached," he laughs. "It's lucky I'm so fond of him."

SENATOR PALPATINE

Palpatine's political savvy serves his purposes well when, as Naboo's representative in the Galactic Senate, he deals with Queen Amidala upon the invasion. He appears nothing but trustworthy in orchestrating Chancellor Valorum's downfall and his own ascendancy to the position.

IAN McDIARMID

McDiarmid is an old hand when it comes to the *Star Wars* world. He first worked with Lucasfilm playing Emperor Palpatine in *Return of the Jedi*. And this is his second time working with *Star Wars* veteran Frank Oz—of Yoda fame—who directed the actor in *Dirty Rotten Scoundrels*. McDiarmid is also no stranger to directing, having directed many plays, including *Don Juan*, *The Rehearsal* and *Siren Song*. McDiarmid is director of the highly acclaimed Almeida Theater in Islington, near London.

YODA

Perhaps foretelling future cataclysmic events, Master Yoda adamantly warns against Qui-Gon's petition to the Jedi Council to train young Anakin as a Jedi Knight. Yoda eventually relents, allowing Obi-Wan to teach the boy the ways of the Force.

FRANK OZ

Born in Hereford, England, Oz began puppeteering at the age of 11. When he was 19, he moved to New York City to join the Muppets, and six years later he ended up on the long-running and highly successful TV series *Sesame Street*, where he became Cookie Monster. Among the many other colorful characters he brought to life on *Sesame Street* are Bert and Grover. He also performed on *The Muppet Show*, playing Animal, Fozzie Bear, Sam the Eagle and his best-known and most-loved character of all, Miss Piggy. Oz joined the *Star Wars* crew for both *The Empire Strikes Back* and *Return of the Jedi*, in which he played the Jedi Master Yoda. But he's not just a highly skilled puppeteer and voice master—he's also a successful director, who's been behind the camera for such entertaining fare as *Little Shop of Horrors*, *Dirty Rotten Scoundrels*, *What About Bob?*, *Housesitter*, *The Indian in the Cupboard*, *In & Out* and *Bowfinger's Big Thing*.

SUPREME CHANCELLOR VALORUM

Attempting to defuse the turmoil created by the greedy Trade Federation's blockade of Naboo, Valorum, head of the Galactic Republic, dispatches two ambassadors to negotiate a settlement. He later becomes an unwitting pawn in Senator Palpatine's plot to unseat and replace the Supreme Chancellor.

TERENCE STAMP

Stamp began his acting career in London, the city where he was born. He was nominated for an Oscar for his 1962 screen debut, as the title character in *Billy Budd*, and three years later took home the Best Actor Award from the Cannes Film Festival for his portrayal as the psychotic kidnapper in *The Collector*. He went on to work with a Who's Who list of directors which includes John Schlesinger, Ken Loach, Pier Paolo Passolini and Federico Fellini. At the height of his fame, Stamp took off to India for a five-year break, occasionally making trips back to England to appear in films. More recently, he showed up to great effect in *The Adventures of Priscilla—Queen of the Desert*, a hit film that did wonders for his career. In addition to his duties as an actor, Stamp has also published the first of three parts of his best-selling autobiography and his first novel.

CAPTAIN PANAKA

Panaka is in charge of Naboo's Royal Security Forces, which are severely outnumbered by the Trade Federation's invading troops. Sworn to safeguard Queen Amidala, he travels with her to Coruscant to seek the Galactic Senate's intervention.

HUGH QUARSHIE

Born in Ghana, Quarshie now lives in England, where he studied politics, philosophy and economics at Oxford, while also acting as co-director of the Oxford and Cambridge Shakespeare Company. After graduating from Oxford, he worked as a journalist, even as he was pursuing an acting career, eventually turning his theater experience into film work on such movies as *Nightbreed*, *Highlander* and *The Dogs of War*. When asked about working with the original *Star Wars* creator as his director on Episode I, Quarshie says, "George gives minimal direction. I think he figures, 'Hey, I've cast good actors. Leave the acting to them.'"

SIO BIBBLE

Bibble is the governor of Theed, the capital of Naboo. A stalwart public official in the face of the encroaching forces of the Trade Federation, he faithfully reports the planet's plight to the Queen during her mission to Coruscant.

OLIVER FORD DAVIES

Working in theater, film and TV for the last 30 years, Oliver Ford Davies also has a Ph.D. from Oxford University and is a trained Shakespearean actor. He has appeared in such films as *Sense and Sensibility*, *Defense of the Realm* and *Paper Mask*, as well as in Lucasfilm's TV series *The Young Indiana Jones Chronicles*.

ROBIN GURLAND
CASTING DIRECTOR

Gurland began her job of finding the right cast for the new *Star Wars* trilogy in July 1995, almost four years before the movie's release. "I've never had such a lead time in casting before," she says. In addition to choosing the film's lead actors, Gurland also had the challenge of finding talent for Episode I's many digital and prosthetic characters.

R2-D2™

QUEEN AMIDALA™

THE POWER OF MYTH

STAR WARS

EPISODE I™

Kellogg's®

FIONN MAC CUMHAILL
MYTH

KING ARTHUR
LEGEND

DARTH MAUL™

QUI-GON JINN™

THE STAR WARS™ POWER OF MYTH™ EXPERIENCE
WEMBLEY EXHIBITION HALL 1 – THURSDAY 1ST JULY TO SUNDAY 11TH JULY

- UNIQUE STAR WARS™ AND MYTHOLOGY EXPO
- EXPERIENCE EPISODE 1 NABOO™ FIGHTER IN ACTION
- ENJOY DARTH VADER™ AND STORMTROOPER™ SHOW
- COMPETE IN STAR WARS™ INTERACTIVE GAMES ARENA
- EXCLUSIVE CINEMATIC EPISODE I PRESENTATION
- FREE STAR WARS™ /KELLOGG'S SAMPLE BAG

TICKETS: ADULTS-£12.50, CHILDREN UNDER 16-£8.50 (SUBJECT TO BKG FEE)
STAR WARS CREDIT CARD HOTLINE: 0181 795 9555
TICKETMASTER: 24HR C/C BOOKING 0171 344 4444 WWW.TICKETMASTER.CO.UK
GROUPS & SCHOOL PARTY DISCOUNTS AVAILABLE: 0181 863 3266
VISIT THE OFFICIAL STAR WARS WEBSITE: WWW.STARWARS.COM

The Script

The First Word

So where exactly does the production of a new *Star Wars* movie begin? It was on November 1, 1994 that George Lucas began writing the script for *Star Wars*: Episode I. Thus began an exciting, if arduous, five-year process that has resulted with *The Phantom Menace*.

Lucas has long let it be known that he conceived the idea *Star Wars* while he was a film student at the University of Southern California in the early 1970s. A few years later, in 1975, he wrote the script for *Star Wars: A New Hope*, which eventually led to the production of the first trilogy, Episodes IV, V and VI. He assured those who longed for more that he had the storylines for the three earlier episodes in his head, and that it would just be a matter of time before the "prequels" were realized as movies, as well.

▲ GEORGE LUCAS WROTE MUCH OF THE SCRIPT FOR *THE PHANTOM MENACE* FROM THE COMFORT OF HOME. WITH PENCIL AND PAPER HE DEVELOPED THE IDEAS THAT HAD BEEN IN HIS HEAD FOR MORE THAN TWO DECADES.

Finally, nearly 20 years after *A New Hope* premiered, Episode I began to take shape. Much had changed in Lucas' life during the intervening two decades. Thanks largely to the *Star Wars* and Indiana Jones trilogies, Lucasfilm had become a major force in the movie industry; along with making film, Lucas oversaw the company's groundbreaking divisions, including Industrial Light & Magic, Skywalker Sound and THX, along with LucasArts Entertainment, Lucas Learning and Lucas Licensing. He also was raising three children and running a non-profit educational foundation. So the decision to dedicate what will end up being the next 10 years of his life to Episodes I, II and III was a critical moment.

"Twenty years ago, it was just a little outline with bits and pieces of story," says Lucas, describing the basic ideas for the events of Episode I as he started committing them to paper. "The outline is pretty much intact for all three prequels, because the structure has to be consistent with the original story. I can interpret it differently, but basically it's the same story. I don't think it will change on the other pictures, either. The story is what the story is. Even though it was written 20 years ago, it's still relevant. It's like going back and working from an old model. In the interpretation of the story, you shift things around. In the original story, Anakin was 12, now he's nine. Things like that you shift, but basically it's still the story of how he becomes a Jedi."

You might imagine that the man who has pioneered modern-day special effects would write the script on a state-of-the-art computer, but actually Lucas uses loose-leaf paper secured in a red binder. "I write with a pencil," he reveals, "and everything I have ever written is in the same three-ring binder. It's a habit. I wrote *American Graffiti* in it, I wrote *Star Wars* in it."

A binder containing some 20-year-old notes and outlines was a nice beginning, but now Lucas had to flesh everything out. He had to develop the characters and their dialogue, he had to realize wondrous new planets and creatures, he had to devise amazing vehicles and other fantastic elements. And everything would have to remain consistent and lead up to the events that audiences already know from *A New Hope*, *Empire* and *Jedi*.

With pencil in hand, he got to work: "A long time ago, in a galaxy far, far away...."

GEORGE LUCAS
Writer, Director, Executive Producer

Like his award-winning special effects people at Industrial Light & Magic, Lucas is also known for being able to get the job done, as millions of *Star Wars* fans will attest to.

"You're always faced with certain limitations," he says, "but it's how well you work in those limitations that defines a really talented filmmaker from someone who's just average. Because everybody has problems. Everybody has limitations. Only some of us learn how to manipulate through those in a more efficient manner than other people. And that's really the secret."

Race-car driving's loss was cinema's gain after Lucas gave up an early passion for competitive auto racing following a serious crash. The course he took to get where he is now saw him attending film school at the University of Southern California, where he turned out several prize-winning short films, including *THX-1138: 4EB/Electronic Labyrinth*. He later shot a longer version of that films for his first feature, while the title was shortened to *THX 1138*.

While his first feature was a cold and technical look at the future, his next was a warm and breezy look at the past—*American Graffiti*. That film about West Coast teens coming of age in the early '60s was made on an impossibly tight budget and went on to reap huge profits, as critics and audiences alike fell in love with it.

It was *American Graffiti* that would allow Lucas the clout he needed to launch his vision out into space with the first of the *Star Wars* series. Three years of preparation went into that first film in the trilogy, but that was nothing compared to the 16 years fans would wait for the next *Star Wars* movie to hit the screen since *Return of the Jedi* landed in theaters everywhere in 1983.

"It's basically my movie that I've been working on for 20 years," Lucas says about Episode I *The Phantom Menace*. And although he professes to being not that keen on technology, preferring to think of himself as a storyteller, he still had to invent the necessary technology to tell his tales.

"When I started the first *Star Wars*," he says, "I had absolutely no idea what we were going to do. Everybody said what we were doing was impossible, and I just blindly went ahead and did it anyway. This time, even though I pushed ILM into frontiers where they'd never gone before, I knew after working with them for 20 years that they could get it done."

THE ART DEPARTMENT

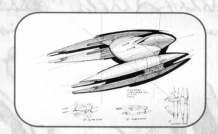

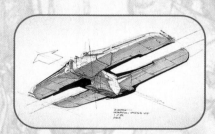

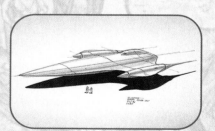

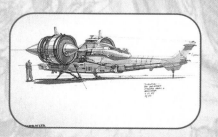

▲ FROM TOP: CONCEPT SKETCHES OF A TRADE FEDERATION DROID STARFIGHTER; TRADE FEDERATION LANDING CRAFT; QUEEN AMIDALA'S ROYAL STARSHIP; PODRACER.

TURNING WORDS INTO IMAGES

Naboo fighters. Gungans. Coruscant. Nute Gunray. Podrace. Watto. Battle droid. Fambaa.

Those are but a handful of the names of people, places and things from *Star Wars*: Episode I *The Phantom Menace*. There are dozens more that emerged from the imagination of George Lucas as he wrote the script for the first of his three prequel films. And while the general look of *Star Wars* was formulated long ago with the original trio of movies, a tremendous challenge awaited Episode I's Art Department. Led by Design Director Doug Chiang, the team had to remain faithful to the former films, yet also travel back in time to imagine what the *Star Wars* universe looked like before the familiar events of Episodes IV, V and VI.

"After I had spent time studying the *Star Wars* style, George came in and told me he wanted something as fresh as Ralph's original work, but different," says Chiang, referring to the seminal concept art developed by Ralph McQuarrie, who along with Joe Johnston and Nilo Rodis-Jamero are generally credited with designing the trilogy as envisioned by Lucas. "We've been saturated in designs derived from the original *Star Wars* look for 20 years now, and George wanted something really new. He said, 'Push the envelope, discover new things.' It was a surprise, but also really exciting. He said, 'I want chrome, sleek shapes, Art Nouveau and Art Moderne.' That's when I realized that this was going to be something new and not just a rework of the earlier material."

Chiang, who had dreamt of such an opportunity ever since first seeing *Star Wars* as a child and eventually going to work for ILM, knew this

would have to be a collaborative effort. So as Lucas transformed his ideas into words, Chiang assembled a specialized gang of design and storyboard artists to help turn those words into images. There was Terryl Whitlatch, for instance, whose background in zoology was perfect for realizing the fantastic creatures of Episode I. Others in the crew— including Iain McCaig, Jay Shuster, Ed Natividad, John Goodson, Benton Jew, Kurt Kaufman, Alex Lindsay, Kevin Baillie, Robert Barnes, Kun Chang, John Duncan, Marc Gabbana, Tony McVey, Richard Miller, Evan Pontoriero, Mark Siegel, Ryan Tudhope, Tony Wright and Jeff Wozniak— pooled their individual talents to design costumes, graphics, environments, vehicles and myriad other visual elements for the film. In the end, they collectively churned out nearly 4,000 pieces of art, including sketches, sculptures, models and production paintings.

The first step was to set some basic parameters that would establish the different look of Episode I. Whereas the Rebels and Imperials in the earlier films were clearly defined by their distinct costumes and vessels, Lucas wanted to "blur the lines, so that when moviegoers see a spaceship [in Episode I] they won't easily know which side that ship represents," Chiang says. "Toward the later times of the classic trilogy, designs become more assembly-line like, with mass-produced aesthetics, hard angles and a machined look. The era of Episode I is more polished, more individualized, even overly designed, but very refined. Vehicles and ships are treated as art forms. Many of them are romantic and elegant. It is a craftsman's era. Every detail is given care. It is kind of like the 1920s and '30s compared to the later 20th century."

During the preproduction phase, Lucas and McCallum would meet every Friday with the Art Department. He came armed with more pages of the script, and they would discuss a range of design concepts, from general color palettes to the specific shape of a starfighter. Then the artists would retreat to their Skywalker Ranch lair, populated with drawing boards and computers, from which would spring more sketches and models to bring to the following week's confab.

Some designs went through an evolutionary process. The Naboo starfighter, for example, began with Lucas simply asking Chiang "to give me a starfighter design," Chiang recalls. Over several weeks' meetings, a variety of concepts were tossed around—some radical, some conservative—before the stylish vessels that Queen Amidala's loyal forces fly against the Trade Federation's invaders were finalized.

At first, the meetings were a bit daunting for the individuals of the art team, who felt pressure to live up to the standards of high quality and design excellence established in the first movies. But before long, a rewarding relationship developed. "Working with George is very rich in

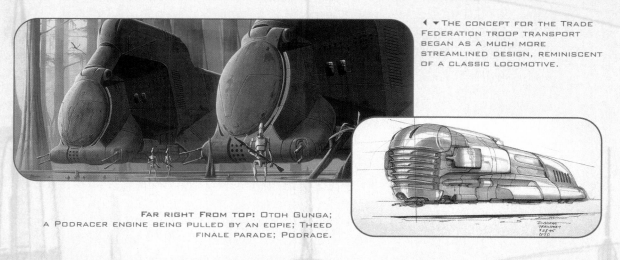

▲ ▼ THE CONCEPT FOR THE TRADE FEDERATION TROOP TRANSPORT BEGAN AS A MUCH MORE STREAMLINED DESIGN, REMINISCENT OF A CLASSIC LOCOMOTIVE.

FAR RIGHT FROM TOP: OTOH GUNGA; A PODRACER ENGINE BEING PULLED BY AN EOPIE; THEED FINALE PARADE; PODRACE.

that not only does he give excellent feedback but he also appreciates great artwork," says Chiang. "You show him a drawing, and he gets it right away, without a lot of explaining."

Creating Coruscant, the ultra-urbanized capital of the Galactic Republic, presented a different type of challenge. The glittering city had a "cameo" in the Special Edition of *Return of the Jedi*, as a computer-generated ILM shot seen during the celebration at the end of the movie, and was imagined somewhat differently by McQuarrie and writer Kevin J. Anderson in *The Illustrated Star Wars Universe*.

"George liked both of those directions, so he wanted to combine both stylistic elements into one image," Chiang explains. "It was like taking Manhattan and scaling it way, way up. All of these buildings are mile- and two-mile-high skyscrapers. Each one of them is several blocks wide at the base. This is the overall view, with flying traffic going throughout the city —a very 3D world."

The Art Department's role in Episode I, however, did not end with the pre-production designs themselves. After that integral stage, Chiang worked with effects supervisors at ILM to be sure that the computer-generated elements were properly merged.

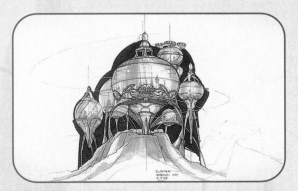

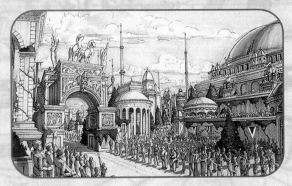

"It's like working on at least five different films," Chiang remarks. "Each world we visit in Episode I has a very unique culture and look. It's a big show."

DOUG CHIANG
DESIGN DIRECTOR

Chiang started his career as a key animator on the *Pee Wee's Playhouse* TV series. He went on to direct and design TV commercials before becoming a Visual Effects Art Director at Industrial Light & Magic, where he worked on such films as *Terminator 2*, *Forrest Gump*, *Jumanji* and the movie for which he won an Academy Award, *Death Becomes Her*.

Donning the Galactic Look

George Lucas' story for Episode I, which takes us to the center of the galaxy and to sophisticated planets whose inhabitants possess majestic wealth, power, political influence and style, necessitated a rich and intricate fashion and costume design. Fulfilling that enormous task were Costume Designer Trisha Biggar, Concept Artist Iain McCaig and a team of creative, hard-working assistants.

The key challenges were the sheer volume of costumes required and the short time frame in which they had to become a reality. In less than a year, Biggar and her core staff of 40 painstakingly designed and assembled more than 1,000 costumes—ranging from Queen Amidala's elaborate dresses to Anakin Skywalker's simple slave outfits. "Our department even manufactured all the accessories, including helmets, headdresses and belt buckles," says Biggar. "They did an incredible job."

Many of Lucas' costume ideas were based on fashions, styles, history and color schemes of various countries in which he is particularly interested, including Japan, Mongolia, China, North Africa and Europe. Yet each costume has a unique look. "Every wardrobe in Episode I has a historical base," explains Biggar, "but we've changed the costumes to keep them from looking recognizably ethnic."

McCaig began creating costume concepts early in the preproduction process. "There wasn't even a script yet," he recalls. "George would describe scenes and characters so we could begin working on some designs."

While giving McCaig and Biggar considerable creative freedom, Lucas was nonetheless very involved in the shaping of his film's fashions. "George is really the ultimate costume designer," says McCaig. "He took what he wanted and guided us where to go." After McCaig completed his design sketches, Biggar turned his work into reality, while adding her own ideas.

The richness, variety and intricacy of the Episode I costumes can be seen on many of the story's characters, but none more so than Queen . Although hesitant to admit to a favorite costume or character, Biggar concedes that she found many opportunities in designing and creating outfits for Queen Amidala, played by Natalie Portman, and her handmaidens. "The costumes for the Queen's planet, Naboo, were very interesting to do, because we printed distinctive designs onto the fabrics," she explains. "We also used various dye techniques, which allowed us to incorporate modern fabrics with antique pieces."

The Queen wears eight costumes throughout the movie. Far fewer were originally planned, but Lucas' desire to expand the universe led to an almost three-fold increase. "George wanted the Queen to have a different outfit every time we see her," Biggar says. Each of those outfits has its own special look. Perhaps the most complex is the Queen's Throne Room dress, which is illuminated by a series of lights around the hem. In keeping with the cultural/historical basis of many of the costumes, it has what Biggar calls "a sort of Chinese Imperial feel" through its scale and silhouette.

The Queen's costumes inspired Biggar and her team to seek out fabrics from all over the world. They even created a few of their own. "We had fabrics woven, painted, dyed—we've done everything you could do to a piece of fabric," recalls Biggar. The Queen's first travel dress was completely handmade and utilizes a spider-web type of fabric that took one person, working five days a week for 10 hours each day, more than a month to make.

Biggar and her team also used several antique pieces. For the Queen's second foreign residence gown, Biggar found a piece from around 1910. "We think it was a dress," she comments, "but it was in so many pieces, we weren't sure what it was." Biggar transformed the piece's motifs into intricate embroidery.

The Queen's battle dress was also time- and work-intensive: It took one person more than a month to complete. It was made from silkworm pods from India, which were woven into a silk net. The Queen's Senate appearance gown, with three layers, is even more intricate. The underdress, which is in orange short silk with a green weave—a 70-year-old fabric—is pleated; the pleats catch the light of the outfit's colors whenever the character moves.

Each of Amidala's costumes had an elaborate headdress. The Senate appearance headdress, which has a Mongolian feel, was the heaviest. The piece was plated in gold to get the right quality of color, then decorated with little jewels. "We felt it was worth the effort, weight and expense of having real gold," says Biggar.

Another headdress was made with an antique piece of beading from an exotic dancer's skirt, circa 1920. Part of it came down onto Portman's forehead; the beads were then draped up over the rest of the headdress, resulting in a bangs-like look. The accompanying dress was based on a Japanese kimono, to which Biggar added her own flourishes. She accentuated the sleeves quite a bit, calling them "penguin sleeves," because they were so rounded they looked somewhat like a penguin.

The retinue of handmaidens who accompany the Queen on her adventures also had to have different outfits. Theirs were always designed with the Queen's outfits in mind, receiving the same attention to detail and style. "We tried to keep the handmaidens in vertical costumes," says Biggar, "with the Queen wearing all kinds of big diagonals and drapery to make her seem larger than life—and her handmaidens small and petite."

While young Anakin Skywalker is a complex character, his costume was one of the simplest. McCaig and Biggar came up with a slave costume that was virtually identical to the one worn by Anakin's future son, Luke Skywalker, in *Star Wars*. For the lightning-paced Podrace, Anakin dons a special helmet and World War I-style goggles. The Podrace headgear was based on a surprisingly terrestrial and everyday source—a child's bicycle helmet. Of course, some new accouterments were placed on top of the helmet to give it a unique look.

Designing the costumes of the Jedi Knights offered different challenges to McCaig and Biggar. The Jedi "look" was familiar to countless *Star Wars* fans. In addition, a principal location in the new film is Tatooine, which was

last seen in *Return of the Jedi*. The planet's recognizable characters and locales provided McCaig and Biggar with the opportunity to maintain fashion continuity from the first three films, while adding their own special touches.

To link those previous looks through to Episode I, Biggar visited the Lucasfilm Archives, where she studied some of the past costumes in detail. Nevertheless, Episode I's story required some new fabrics or design modifications. In a departure from the previous films, all Jedi costumes were made of silk, linen or very fine wool. Some changes were also made in the undergarments to the original costumes; they were now more suitable and wearer-friendly for the new film's acrobatic fight and stunt scenes and lightsaber battles.

One aspect of the Jedi look that wasn't carried over from the other *Star Wars* films was hair. Whereas Sir Alec Guinness did not have a particular hair style when the distinguished British actor played Obi-Wan more than 20 years ago, McGregor's younger version of the character has distinct locks, especially with the single, long braid that designates Obi-Wan as an apprentice Jedi. In contrast, his mentor, Qui-Gon, wears his hair much longer.

"I'm going into areas that I carefully avoided in the first three films," says George Lucas, speaking of the overall look of *The Phantom Menace*. "There are a lot more costumes, a lot more design work, a lot more hairdos." Indeed, the director jokes, "If they didn't like my hairdos in *Star Wars*, they're really not going to like them in this one. It'll drive them nuts."

TRISHA BIGGAR

COSTUME DESIGNER

Costumes have always played a big part in the *Star Wars* saga, and for the beginning of his latest trilogy, George Lucas recruited Biggar to design the costumes. He was already familiar with her work through their collaboration on the *Young Indiana Jones Chronicles* TV series. Trained at the Wimbledon School of Art, Biggar began her career in the theater before moving on to such films as *Silent Scream*, *Wild West* and *Moll Flanders*.

IAIN McCAIG

CONCEPT ARTIST

A filmmaker, concept designer and art director, prior to Episode I, McCaig served as Senior Character Designer on *Frankenstein*, as well as principle designer on Francis Ford Coppola's *Pinocchio* and Sony Pictures' *Dinotopia*. As a storyboard artist and concept designer at ILM, McCaig worked on *Hook*, *Terminator 2*, *Star Trek IV* and *The Young Indiana Jones Chronicles*. In March 1998, his first foray into the world of directing, *The Face*, debuted at the Santa Barbara Film Festival and won the Houston International Film Festival's Gold Medal for Best Family Film. McCaig is also a widely published illustrator. His work includes book and record covers, limited-edition prints, posters, advertising and children's books.

THE MODEL UNIVERSE

By Mark Cotta Vaz

▲ AN ELABORATELY
DETAILED MINI
VERSION OF THEED,
THE EXOTIC CAPITAL
OF NABOO, WAS
CONSTRUCTED BY THE
MODEL-MAKING TEAM.

Star Wars model shop veteran Steve Gawley has perfectly summed up the energy of Industrial Light & Magic during the making of the first movie: "We were young, enthusiastic and making these neat spaceships."

Gawley has recalled how they bought supplies at a government surplus store, how the spartan *Star Wars* screening room had a screen, a projector and busted furniture ("early Goodwill" according to Gawley). But despite such humble beginnings, that original *Star Wars* shop still managed to push the proverbial envelope, replacing the traditional wood, plaster and steel materials of their craft with machined aluminum and plastics.

Today, in the digital era, model making was supposed to be doomed. Even at the outset of ILM's production on *The Phantom Menace*, much of the anticipatory buzz was about digital backlots and CG actors. However, to paraphrase the old saying, reports of the death of model making have been greatly exaggerated. For *Phantom*, ILM's model shop had 100 separate

◄ AMONG THE DOZENS OF FULL-SCALE MODELS MADE FOR EPISODE I WERE SEBULBA'S PODRACER AND SEVERAL BATTLE DROIDS.

model projects, ranging from 10 fiberglass battle droids used on the live-action set at Leavesden (each, at full-size, nearly six and a half feet tall) to model vehicles and miniature environments that could be filmed, scanned into a computer and fused with CG effects.

"I'd say this film was seven to eight times bigger than our largest previous show," says Gawley, who supervised the entire effort. "There were at least 20 projects going during any one week. The volume of work was just huge. That was the biggest challenge. So we reinvented how to do things quicker and at less cost."

The Model Shop effort helmed by Gawley included the delegation of specific projects to the leadership of eight chief model makers (including trilogy veterans Lorne Peterson and Charlie Bailey), a team of 60 to 80 skilled model makers, painters (a crew headed by Steve Walton, which literally painted on Lucas' famed "used universe" look of wear-and-tear to model vehicles, spaceships and buildings) and set designer William Beck, who drew up architectural designs for taking concepts to creation.

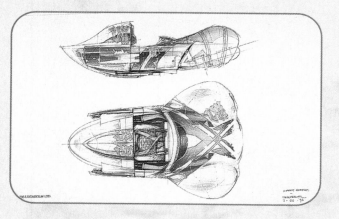

◀ ▲ THE MODEL-MAKING PROCESS TYPICALLY EVOLVED FROM PREPRODUCTION SKETCHES RENDERED BY THE ART DEPARTMENT.

GAWLEY'S CREW CONSTRUCTED A MODEL OF C-3PO, WHICH WAS OPERATED BY A PUPPETTEER IN FRONT OF A GREENSCREEN. ▼

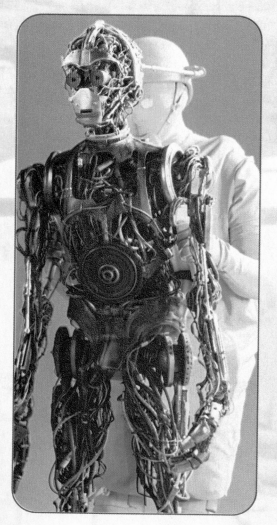

Gawley notes his shop was also aided by a new generation of "cool tools," from a laser cutter to a CNC ("computer numerical controlled") milling machine for rapidly and accurately cutting materials into specific designs. A particular advantage of the CNC, Gawley observes, was it could utilize data from CG models to create physical versions, giving filmmakers the option to seamlessly cut between CG and model versions. "We could take the digital information on the Queen's ship, put it in our CNC and make an exact copy, providing a true match between digital and [physical] three-dimensional," Gawley says. "I think there's now a fantastic marriage between models and digital. Practical plus digital equals the future."

That marriage allowed the model shop to create miniature sets—from sections of the desert Podrace route and the hallways of the Theed palace—to augment or extend largely virtual environments. Gawley's modelers built a physical C-3PO that was traditionally puppeteered on the set—with the puppet master digitally erased from the footage. CG-built Podracers were based on the physical models constructed at one-eighth scale (two to four feet long) from silicon molds and lightweight foam castings.

Theed was perhaps the ultimate fusion of digital and traditional, a creation that took model making to the level of high art. Like something out of an Arabian night's dream, the model shop's exotic towers, archways and minarets provided the setting for some fantastic illusions, including the victory procession of CG Gungans and live-action characters.

◄ Motion-control cameras were used to shoot a model of a Trade Federation battleship.

To realize Theed, a crew of about 40 worked nearly three months to produce 68 separate buildings, each an average of three to four feet tall. Both Theed and the Gungan capital of Otoh Gunga, another exotic city built by the model makers, could be assembled and shot outdoors on a large platform holding a rotatable table built at ILM's Marin County facility. The set-up was so big, the production purchased a quonset hut-shaped airplane hangar to roll over the stage at night to protect the exquisite models from the elements.

After two years on Episode I, and mere months before the film's release, Gawley was anticipating seeing a new *Star Wars* film in a theater. "I'm really excited," he smiled, and it seemed like those days many years ago when he and the rest of a plucky band of fledgling ILMers began to create the universe.

"And this time around I have two kids," Gawley smiled, "a boy and a girl, ages 10 and eight, to share the experience with. There's just an amazing amount of world he [Lucas] is showing audiences. I also think the timing is great. The world is ready to see *Star Wars* again."

▲ Sketches of parts of Podracers were converted into models.

◄ Steve Gawley (far left), Doug Chiang (center) and John Knoll discuss the particulars of a battle droid model.

PREPRODUCTION

The Creature Shop

Plot is important in *Star Wars*. So are creatures. For all the mythical storytelling, pitting the human (or at least humanoid) forces of good and evil against one another in fantastic worlds and situations, the movies' appeal is also reflected in their out-of-this-world characters: Yoda, Chewbacca, Jabba the Hutt, Salacious Crumb, Nien Nunb, Gamorrean guards, Oola, Jawas and a gaggle of other aliens. And then there's the cantina scene in *A New Hope*, which is as much a cinematic landmark as Rick's café in *Casablanca*, Xanadu in *Citizen Kane* or Tara in *Gone with the Wind*—though with its outrageous denizens from across the galaxy, maybe a nod to the Delta House's motley crew in *Animal House* is more apt.

The Phantom Menace raises the creature bar to incredible heights. The movie is populated with otherworldly characters both familiar and foreign, as George Lucas returns to Tatooine, Luke Skywalker's home planet, and visits a new place called Naboo. Yoda's back, and so are Wookiees. But we're also introduced to Gungans, Dugs, Neimoidians and Toydarians.

▲ THE MODEL SHOP AT LEAVESDEN STUDIOS WAS FILLED WITH AN ASSORTMENT OF OTHERWORLDLY CREATURE HEADS, ARMS, HANDS AND VARIOUS BODY PARTS.

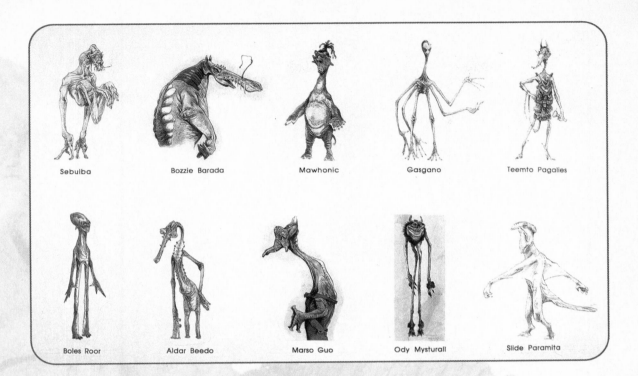

Sebulba

Bozzie Barada

Mawhonic

Gasgano

Teemto Pagalies

Boles Roor

Aldar Beedo

Marso Guo

Ody Mysturall

Slide Paramita

▲ THE PROCESS FOR DESIGNING CREATURES BEGAN WITH CONCEPT DRAWINGS GENERATED BY THE EPISODE I ART DEPARTMENT. NOTE THE PRELIMINARY NAMES

▼ THE ITHORIAN SPECIES, KNOWN AS HAMMERHEADS IN STAR WARS, IS REPRESENTED IN THE GALACTIC SENATE.

So who comes up with these weird wonders of the *Star Wars* universe? Well, like most everything else there, the basic concepts are born in Lucas' fertile imagination before he hands them over to his various creative teams, whose collective job it is to bring them to filmic life. In this case, the process began with Terryl Whitlatch. If it wasn't a creature from one of the past three films, for which masks already existed within the vast Lucasfilm Archives, Doug Chiang, Iain McCaig and Whitlatch generated hundreds of drawings and sketches based on Lucas' script and copious notes. Some of them were then realized by Industrial Light & Magic as computer-generated entities—the Tatooine junk dealer Watto, for instance—while others were the handmade fabrications of the Live-Action Creature Effects Department, headed by Nick Dudman.

◀ A YOUNGER YODA, BASED ON THE ORIGINAL PUPPET FROM *THE EMPIRE STRIKES BACK*, WAS FABRICATED IN THE CREATURE SHOP, PIECE BY PIECE.

"When Producer Rick McCallum started talking to me about Episode I, I had assumed that it all was going to be computer-generated," says Dudman, who launched his film career on *The Empire Strikes Back*. But after reading the script and meeting with Chiang, that assumption changed. Lucasfilm gradually determined that certain creatures would be better presented physically rather than digitally, thus necessitating Dudman's expertise in animatronics, prosthetic make-up and puppetry. "They decided that Yoda would be a puppet and made the same way he was before," says the Creature Effects Supervisor. "Then all these other characters started surfacing, where they said, 'We don't need to CG it, so why are we?' And the people at ILM were more than happy if we suggested that something could be animatronic.

"I think it's important never to lose sight of the fact that just because the technology is changing, with new materials, new processes and new equipment, we're still making rubber heads that we put on people," Dudman says in support of traditional effects. "It's important not to lose the flavor of what went before."

Therein lied the ultimate mission for Dudman and his team: to cohesively blend the old with the new, utilizing both archival elements and modern technology. "The variety of work was quite extreme," Dudman says. "We had to decide which characters would be approached in which way." If a creature was only going to appear in the background, prosthetic make-up might be the way to go, but if it was a prominent character featured in close-ups, an animatronic might work best.

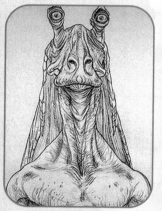

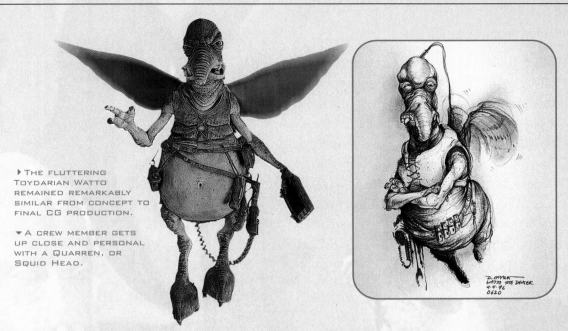

▶ THE FLUTTERING
TOYDARIAN WATTO
REMAINED REMARKABLY
SIMILAR FROM CONCEPT TO
FINAL CG PRODUCTION.

▼ A CREW MEMBER GETS
UP CLOSE AND PERSONAL
WITH A QUARREN, OR
SQUID HEAD.

Yoda's appearance in *The Phantom Menace* provides a prime example of such melding, as well as a poignant blast from the past. Dudman's job on *Empire* was to assist legendary make-up artist Stuart Freeborn on characters including the ancient little Jedi Master. "The original Yoda, built in 1979, was a complete prototype," Dudman remembers. "Nobody involved had any idea how to build it. It was a case of try this and see what happens."

Of course, what happened was phenomenal, as Yoda, an animatronic puppet operated by Muppet master Frank Oz, became one of *Star Wars*' most enduring characters. In *Phantom*, Yoda is more than 30 years younger (he's nearly 900 in *Empire*!), so what more would Dudman have to do to that puppet than perhaps shed a few decades' wrinkles? "When we got the original out of the Archives, and I showed it to Chris Barton, my Animatronics Supervisor, we said, basically, you couldn't improve it. What we could do, though, was make it more streamlined or slick."

Empire Yoda was made from foam latex, an opaque material; *Phantom* Yoda is made from silicone. "It's heavier, but it gives a translucency and a reality and a subtlety of movement that foam just can't do," Dudman explains. "And after discussions with Frank Oz, Chris altered some of the ways the puppet works." In *Empire*, Oz found it difficult to manually operate Yoda's expressive eyebrows with his fingers, so "we've made that radio-controlled," says Dudman. "And we've added a smile mechanism. But the actual lip-synching is still done by Frank. I said, 'Let's not try to design character into a mechanical gadget when we have Frank Oz to do it.'"

Also returning to action in Episode I is Chewbacca—well, actually it's just a Wookiee suit from the Archives that's been used lately for Chewie's public appearances at events. "George decided that in the Senate sequence, where there are all these pods of different creatures and species swinging about, it would be great to have a group of Wookiees there," Dudman reports. "They wanted three Wookiee suits out of the Archives, but we decided to shoot one three times. We added a great deal of white hair to the head and body, and did one pass with the camera. We took some of the white hair out and did another pass. Then we took most of the white hair out and did a third pass."

Numerous surplus creature costumes were resurrected from the Lucasfilm Archives. Their inclusion, however, was more arbitrary. "We just pinned up pictures of a lot of the original creatures on a board," Dudman says, reconstructing a session with Director Lucas. "I said to George, 'OK, how many do you want, and which ones?'" They agreed on about a dozen, including a Hammerhead, a Rodian, an Ishi Tib and a Squid Head.

Dudman's crew also produced a number of species new to the *Star Wars* environment, based on the Art Department's concept drawings. They ranged from small alien frogs to the huge Horox Ryyder. (The most prominent gathering of creatures in Episode I—the movie's cantina scene, if you will—occurs during the Podrace.)

No doubt, the most unique challenge was Jar Jar Binks. He's seen in the film as a completely CG character, but getting the mischievous Gungan to that point combined the computer talents at ILM with the material effects in the Creature Shop. "Jar Jar was a different approach, for everything," says Dudman. "He was originally purely CG— nothing to do with us at all." Then Lucas and McCallum decided they needed something physical to walk through scenes during filming, to

ISHI TIB

HOROX RYYDER

NIKTO

JEDI PLO KOON

provide a lighting reference for ILM's subsequent digital renderings and also to give the actors a real "character" to react to. "We created a suit and a very odd-looking head piece that Ahmed Best wore, which put the eyes on Jar Jar at the correct height," says Dudman.

Producer Rick McCallum describes how it all worked on the sets. "Basically, what happened was that Ahmed came in, and we rehearsed the scene with him. We did four or five takes until the actors felt comfortable and knew where his eye line was. Then, once we had that take—we actually shot that as a reference for ILM, in terms of attitude and position—we shot a blank plate without Ahmed. He was off-camera, giving the lines. The actors knew where they were supposed to be looking and how they were interacting with him. Then we used that plate to later animate."

Jar Jar is a groundbreaking effect, adds Lucas, one that has emerged from ILM's past achievements. "He is a truly synthetic cyber-character," he says. "The CG ghosts did some acting in *Casper*, and we made very lifelike creatures in *Jurassic Park*, but nobody has ever made a lifelike creature that acts, that has a performance and is a regular character."

The Phantom Menace is destined to set a variety of precedents in filmmaking, and its pantheon of creatures is sure to be among them. Nick Dudman will head the list of names credited for creating them, though he is quick to emphasize the entire team's efforts and his role as leader. "When you're running a large crew—and this one was 55 people—it's no good to stand over them. I see my job as gently nudging people in the direction I want them to go, but making them feel confident that their contributions are being recognized, and that their skills are being used to their best advantage. It works very well."

RODIAN

WOOKIEE

BITH   BARADA

NICK DUDMAN
CREATURE EFFECTS SUPERVISOR
Dudman broke into the physical effects business working on Yoda in *The Empire Strikes Back*. Other Lucasfilm productions he contributed to include *Return of the Jedi*, *Willow* and *Indiana Jones & the Last Crusade*. He also worked on *Superman II*, *Legend*, *Interview with the Vampire* and *The Fifth Element*. Dudman's company, Pigs Might Fly, markets a proprietary prosthetic material called Dermplast.

READY... SET...
ACTION!
Leavesden Studios - England

It was almost exactly 20 years after the first *Star Wars* movie premiered when George Lucas began filming the fourth one. From May 1977 to June 1997, however, so much had transpired. *Star Wars* and its sequels, *The Empire Strikes Back* (1980) and *Return of the Jedi* (1983), had collectively become a cultural and entertainment phenomenon. Legions of loyal fans longed for more —especially knowing that Lucas indeed had more story to tell—but it wouldn't be until the early 1990s that he somewhat sated them with novels, comics and games which extrapolated upon the trilogy's events. A second generation of toys and collectibles would further fuel fans' burning desire, and then they went ballistic with the official announcement in 1995 that a new trio of movies would at long last be made. Finally, as if any more groundwork needed to be laid, in early '97 Lucasfilm released the *Star Wars Trilogy Special Edition*, enhanced versions of the original films. They were a huge sensation, not only among longtime fans but also younger generations, who saw them in the theater for the very first time.

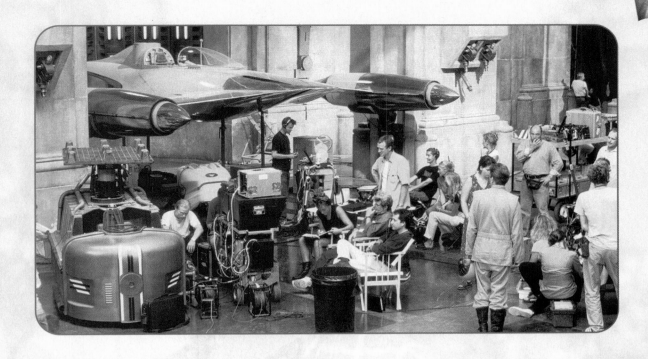

◄ LEAVESDEN STUDIOS WAS BUILT AROUND AN OLD AIRCRAFT FACTORY. AMONG THE SETS BUILT FOR *THE PHANTOM MENACE* WERE THE NABOO STARFIGHTER HANGAR AND THE DROID POWER GENERATOR ABOARD THE FEDERATION BATTLESHIP.

While the 20-year mark was a convenient coincidence, it was also the point at which Lucas was entirely ready to reopen his saga and present the "back story" to the tales of Luke Skywalker, Darth Vader, Obi-Wan Kenobi and other people, places and things in the known *Star Wars* universe. Lucas needed that time to develop and perfect the critical moviemaking techniques necessary to relay on the silver screen the prequels he had so long envisioned.

"When I started the first *Star Wars*, everybody said what we were doing was impossible, and I just went ahead and did it anyway," Lucas says, recalling the technological challenges he and his special effects crew faced then. "This time, even though I'm pushing Industrial Light & Magic into frontiers it's never gone into before, I know after working with them for 20 years that they can do it."

So now the script was written and the myriad design concepts were in place. From that foundation, costumes were being fabricated, models constructed and creatures conceived. Actors had been cast and various production crews—from set builders to camera operators, many of whom had worked together for McCallum on the *Young Indiana Jones Chronicles* TV series—were hired. It was time to start the cameras rolling on the live-action scenes, which would eventually be integrated with hundreds of ILM visual effects in post-production. This filming phase would last all through the summer of '97 and be based in England, with brief, but intense remote shoots in Italy and Tunisia.

Principal photography for the first three *Star Wars* movies was done at England's Elstree Studios outside of London. Lucas, who has generally remained outside the Hollywood mainstream, enjoyed the crews and facilities in England, and keeping his distance from the U.S. media allowed him a desired

▲ AFTER CONSTRUCTING A
SET, SUCH AS THIS ONE FOR
THE EXTERIOR OF THEED,
PROPS WERE ADDED.

veil of secrecy. Elstree, though, was not large enough for the elaborate sets he planned to erect for *The Phantom Menace.* McCallum wanted raw space, and plenty of it. He found it in Leavesden, a quaint hamlet north of London where a former aircraft facility had been converted into a movie-production facility.

▲ HERE IS ONE
OF THE JEDI'S
TESTING SCREENS.

Leavesden Studios is a 286-acre complex of nondescript, brick office buildings, gigantic hangars, an abandoned airstrip and lots of wide-open spaces. Roll-Royce used to build aircraft engines there, then a few years ago an outfit called Millennium Group Ltd. bought it and retrofitted it for moviemaking. Now it was to become the center of that galaxy far, far away.

"I was looking for a big place we could turn into our own studio," says Episode I Producer Rick McCallum. "It's not luxurious, but it has 800,000 square feet of working space, which we were able to convert into eight sound stages, a huge area that we turned into a workshop for set construction and the largest backlot of any studio in the world. It's the ideal place to shoot. We were able to film and build at the same time, effortlessly and seamlessly."

DIRECTOR GEORGE LUCAS DIDN'T
ACTUALLY OPERATE THE CAMERAS, BUT
HE WOULD OFTEN GET A PREVIEW OF
WHAT HE WAS ABOUT TO SHOOT. ▶

THE GOLDEN OLDIES...

RELIVE THE EXCITEMENT!
OFFICIAL SOUVENIR FILM MAGAZINES

If you're a film fan, here's an opportunity not to be missed! We have in stock, limited numbers of collectible Souvenir and Poster Magazines and Comics of classic films from the last few years. These magazines and comics bring you all the behind-the-scenes low-down on some great films.

ORDER YOURS NOW – SUPPLIES ARE LIMITED!

ORDER FORM

ALL ORDERS TO TITAN MUST BE MADE IN £ STERLING
To calculate total cost add up the price of the magazine and the postage and packing (Magazine price + Postage and Packing = Cost)

Postage and Packing
Magazines priced as shown in order form plus

COUNTRY	P&P PER MAGAZINE
UK	£1.00
EIRE	£1.50

Payment must be made in £ sterling

Name_____

Address_____

_____

Postcode_____ Country_____

I enclose a cheque (UK only)/IMO/PO made payable to Titan Books for the total cost. Payment must be made in £ sterling. Do not send cash.

Or Charge my ☐ Visa ☐ Mastercard ☐ American Express
☐ Switch*/Delta*

Card Number

Expiry date_____

*Switch and Delta available in the UK only. If paying by Switch/Delta please include the following:

Switch issue number:_____ Start Date:_____

Signature:_____ Date:_____

To receive your magazines simply fill in the order form (photocopies are acceptable) and post it to:

Golden Oldies Back Issues
Titan Magazines
c/o Bowden House
36 Northampton Road
Market Harborough, Leics
England LE16 9HE

Alternatively, telephone your order through on **+44 (0)-1858 433 169** quoting reference GOBI or fill out the form and fax it to us on **+44 (0)-1858 433 715**. If not using the order form please ensure to include all the above information. Office hours are 9:00-5:00 p.m. Mon-Fri.

☐ Tick here if you do not wish to receive details of any special offer or new products.

GOBI 1 2 3 4 5 6 7 8 9 10

No	COLLECTABLE MOVIE MAGAZINES	Price	P&P	Cost
	The Avengers Souvenir Magazine		£4.00	
	Batman Forever Souvenir Magazine		£4.00	
	Batman Forever Poster Magazine 1		£3.00	
	Batman Forever Poster Magazine 2		£3.00	
	Batman Forever Poster Magazine 3		£3.00	
	Batman Forever Poster Magazine 4		£3.00	
	Batman Forever Poster Magazine 5		£3.00	
	Batman Forever Poster Magazine 6		£3.00	
	Batman Returns Poster Magazine 1		£3.00	
	Batman Returns Poster Magazine 2		£3.00	
	Batman Returns Poster Magazine 3		£3.00	
	Batman & Robin Souvenir Magazine		£4.00	
	Batman & Robin Poster Magazine 1		£3.00	
	Batman & Robin Poster Magazine 2		£3.00	
	Batman & Robin Poster Magazine 3		£3.00	
	Barb Wire Souvenir Magazine		£4.00	
	The Crow Souvenir Magazine		£3.00	
	Dr Moreau Souvenir Magazine		£3.00	
	Dragonheart Souvenir Magazine		£3.50	
	Godzilla Souvenir Magazine		£4.00	
	Goldeneye Souvenir Magazine		£5.00	
	Independence Day Souvenir Magazine		£4.00	
	Judge Dredd Poster Magazine 1		£3.00	
	Judge Dredd Poster Magazine 2		£3.00	
	Judge Dredd Poster Magazine 3		£3.00	
	Judge Dredd Poster Magazine 4		£3.00	
	Judge Dredd Poster Magazine 5		£3.00	
	Lost in Space Souvenir Magazine		£4.00	
	Spawn Souvenir Magazine		£4.00	
	Spawn Poster Magazine		£3.00	
	Star Trek: 1st Contact Poster Magazine 1		£3.00	
	Star Trek: 1st Contact Poster Magazine 2		£3.00	
	Star Trek: 1st Contact Poster Magazine 3		£3.00	
	Star Trek: Insurrection Poster Magazine 1		£3.00	
	Star Trek: Insurrection Poster Magazine 2		£3.00	
	Star Trek: Insurrection Poster Magazine 3		£3.00	
	Star Trek: Insurrection Poster Magazine 4		£3.00	
	Star Wars Original Trilogy Heroes Poster Magazine		£5.00	
	Star Wars Original Trilogy Villains Poster Magazine		£5.00	
	Star Wars Special Edition Commenorative Sovenir Magazine		£9.00	
	Tomorrow Never Dies Souvenir Magazine		£4.00	
	Twister Souvenir Magazine		£3.00	
	TOTAL COSTS MAGAZINES			

COLLECTIBLE COMICS	Price	Cost
Batman & Robin Comic 1	£3.00	
Lost World Comic 1	£2.00	
Lost World Comic 2	£2.00	
Lost World Comic 3	£2.00	
Lost World Comic 4	£2.00	
Space Above & Beyond Comic 1	£3.00	
Starship Troopers Comic 1	£2.00	
Starship Troopers Comic 2	£2.00	
TOTAL COSTS COMICS		

TOTAL COSTS
(Incl Postage & Packing)

By the time actual filming commenced, Leavesden Studios was humming with activity. Nearly 65 sets would ultimately be built, indoors and outdoors, and many were already complete or under construction. The various buildings housed administrative offices, design studios and workshops for making props, droids, vehicles, animatronics and creatures.

The sets were constructed inside the massive old hangars under the direction of Production Designer Gavin Bocquet. "My job is to interpret George Lucas' ideas and convert them into some sort of visual form," says Bocquet, whose past Lucasfilm credits include *Jedi*, *Radioland Murders* and *The Young Indiana Jones Chronicles*. "We produced any constructed background that you see behind the actors, whether it was an in-studio set or on location, including props and set dressing. In short, we dealt with any inanimate objects." In total, Bocquet and the designers and crafts people who worked with him built 65 sets.

▲ THE EXTERIOR OF THE SET FOR THE JEDI COUNCIL MEETING ON CORUSCANT.

GAVIN BOCQUET

Production Designer

A graduate of Newcastle Polytechnic and The Royal College of Art, Bocquet began his film career as an art department draftsman on *The Elephant Man* and *Return of the Jedi*. He was promoted to Art Director for *Empire of the Sun* and was hired as the Production Designer on Lucasfilm's TV series *The Young Indiana Jones Chronicles*, a role he also assumes for Episode I.

▲ THE WINDOWS OF THE INTERIOR OF PALPATINE'S CHAMBERS WERE SHOT WITH BLUESCREEN; CG VIEWS OF CORUSCANT WERE LATER ADDED BY ILM.

"The development of every environment was sort of an organic process," Bocquet explains. "If you look back at the Art Department's early sketches and models, many things changed a certain amount from the initial concepts. Gradually the process moved along, through sketches, reference photographs or location photographs, toward something that was much more defined. Each set followed that pattern."

One of Star Wars' enduring qualities is the ability to take moviegoers to strange new worlds which, although they may exist in the fantasy realm, are still rooted in what's real and familiar—be it the deserts and canyons of Tatooine or the arboreal environs of Endor. "The audience needs something to key into, an air of reality," Bocquet asserts.

KENNY BAKER (FRONT) AWAITS HIS NEXT SCENE AS R2-D2.
▼

DAVID TATTERSALL

DIRECTOR OF PHOTOGRAPHY

Tattersall studied at Britain's National Film School, where he specialized in working behind the camera. His highly regarded student films culminated with *Metropolis Apocalypse* being accepted in the Cannes Film Festival. He's previously worked with George Lucas on the *Young Indiana Jones Chronicles* TV series and was on the set for *Con Air* and *The Green Mile*.

ON LOCATION

FULL-SIZE NABOO STARFIGHTERS WERE USED IN HANGAR SCENES, WHILE SCALE MODELS WERE SHOT WITH MOTION-CONTROL CAMERAS FOR SPACE BATTLE SEQUENCES.

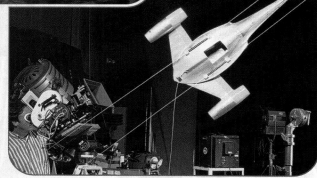

In that respect, creating the underwater city of Otoh Gunga was a particularly challenging task for the Production Designer. "There were no key reference points to any type of underwater city," says Bocquet. "It was just a feel thing between us and George. The fun part was experimenting and working toward the time when we shot Otoh Gunga, hoping that we got the right answer."

They got the answer, all right, with an undersea fantasy world protected by series of vast bubble-like membranes. The exterior views of the Gungans' watery city are actually digital masterpieces built in ILM computers, not wood and plaster sets in a hangar at Leavesden, though the interior scenes were assembled in the studio.

Whether the exteriors for Episode I were generated in a computer or shot on location in England, Tunisia or Italy, most of the interiors were fabricated at Leavesden: Anakin and Shmi's slave quarters, the cockpit of Amidala's Royal Starship, the Naboo fighter hangar, the Jedi Council room, the generator core aboard the Trade Federation droid control ship and many more. The process of building each set began with Art Department renderings, which were the basis for a small, foam-core model, which reverted back to two dimensions as blueprints, which were handed over to Gavin Bocquet's set-construction crews. And while erecting floors, walls, windows and other fundamental components was a gargantuan undertaking, so too was dressing the sets and filling them with props.

After Bocquet's crew completed the hammer-and-nail phase on a set, Set Decorator Peter Walpole and his team got down to the business of adding the finishing touches, from furniture to weapons. Because they were functioning in the fantasy world, it wasn't as easy as ordering things from a catalog or going on a shopping spree at the mall. Many of the props and set dressings were cobbled together from real-world bits and pieces of this and that.

Walpole and Prop Master Ty Teiger operated out of a huge storeroom at Leavesden, filled with shelf after shelf of scrap metal, plastic parts, defunct computers and hundreds of other odds and ends gathered from junkyards, airfields, even a medical equipment warehouse. Old aircraft seats were retrofitted into a starship's cockpit, computer parts became wall panels in Anakin's bedroom, plastic barrels were turned into chairs. Don't look too closely for such tricks of the trade, though. The pros at Leavesden diligently disguised their handiwork in an effort to make everything blend in perfectly.

ON LOCATION

When Lucas sat down in his director's chair in June 1997, it marked the first time in more than two decades that he was at the helm of a movie. He directed *Star Wars*, but turned over the reins to Irvin Kershner for *Empire* and Richard Marquand for *Jedi*. Lucas was now facing a daunting, three-month ordeal that would result in 65 days of shooting, more than 3,700 setups and 1.3 million feet of film. And that was just the live-action portion of *The Phantom Menace*, to which ILM would add its hundreds of elements in post-production and Lucas and Editor Paul Martin Smith would whittle down to two hours and 10 minutes of running time.

"I just never had the time before to do it," says Lucas when asked about directing again. "It was interesting to go back and direct. It was much more intense than what I've been doing—running companies, raising kids and all kinds of other things." Intense is putting it mildly, considering his days started at around five in the morning and often wouldn't end until past midnight.

Adding another degree of difficulty, the filming of Episode I, as with many movies, was not done in sequence with the script, so maintaining continuity from scene to scene required tremendous coordination among the production's various departments. And because special effects would be integrated into nearly every shot, ILM's John Knoll sat right beside Lucas. Meanwhile, Second Unit Director Roger Christian was supervising another film crew that would shoot incidental close-ups, street scenes and other random bits. It was a wild

THE INTERIOR SETS FOR ANAKIN AND SHMI SKYWALKER'S SLAVE QUARTERS ON TATOOINE WERE AMONG THE DOZENS CONSTRUCTED AT LEAVESDEN STUDIOS.

scene at Leavesden, yet there was an obvious energy and camaraderie that emanated from the top. "With George at the helm, it seemed to have the same feel as the first one, as *Star Wars*, which is great," says Christian, a set decorator on the original film.

Producer McCallum echoes Christian's sentiments. "George had 20 years to plan this film, and it showed on the set. He knows what he wants, and he gets it. He is quiet and self-assured, and the crew admires him for it. Although we had an extraordinary amount of work to do, his confidence proved to be contagious and the production went rather smoothly."

And ending much speculation surrounding Episodes II and III, McCallum will surely brighten fans' futures with the news that Lucas "will be directing the next films, as well."

Nonetheless, this will be Leavesden's one and only *Star Wars* gig. During post-production, Lucas and McCallum announced that the next two episodes will be filmed at the new Fox Studios in Sydney, Australia. The truth is, though, that when it comes to *Star Wars*, all the world is George Lucas' stage.

FIT FOR A QUEEN
On Location - Caserta, Italy

Queen Amidala plays a major role in *The Phantom Menace* as the young monarch who must forcefully deal with the Trade Federation's space blockade and armed invasion of her peaceful planet Naboo. She succeeds in doing so not only through her regal status but also the valiant efforts of her duel persona, when she disguises herself as the queen's handmaiden Padmé Naberrie.

Besides heroic endeavors, Amidala is remarkable for her opulent wardrobe and the magnificent palace in Naboo's capital, Theed, from where she rules. We never got to see Princess Leia's royal digs on Alderaan in *A New Hope* before Grand Moff Tarkin ordered that the entire planet be obliterated to demonstrate the awesome power of the Death Star. Theed, though, is prominently displayed in all its palatial splendor in Episode I.

▲ THE ROYAL PALACE OF CASERTA, BUILT IN ITALY MORE THAN 500 YEARS AGO, WAS THE IDEAL LOCATION FOR THE REGAL RESIDENCE OF QUEEN AMIDALA.

▲ WITH THE COOPERATION OF THEIR HOSTS IN CASERTA, GEORGE LUCAS AND HIS FILM CREW WERE ALLOWED TO SHOOT SCENES INSIDE THE PALACE.

The presentation on film of the city and its spectacular palace was achieved on four fronts: Some scenes were shot on interior and exterior sets built at Leavesden Studios; ILM added a wide array of computer-generated elements; Steve Gawley's model-making department built an incredible miniature of the palace and its grounds; and the cast and crew traveled to Italy to shoot on location.

The Italian sojourn was in the city of Caserta, 45 minutes northeast of Naples. There, Charles VII, the king of France from 1422-61, built the wondrous Reggia di Caserta, or Royal Palace at Caserta. Charles wanted a residence to rival his ancestors' palaces at Versailles and Escorial, and commissioned a complex of buildings and gardens that overshadowed both. The palace itself consists of 1,200 exquisite rooms; a majestic, 116-step staircase, leading to the extravagant royal apartments, was carved from a single, massive block of stone. The opulent gardens feature an abundance of plantings, plus ponds, fountains and various buildings.

ON LOCATION

GEORGE LUCAS HAD
THE CAPABILITY TO
DIGITALLY CREATE
THE SETS FOR THE
QUEEN'S PALACE,
BUT HE OPTED TO
UTILIZE THE
REMARKABLE ROOMS
AT CASERTA.

"When we started to scout for locations, we looked in various countries and cities," says Rick McCallum, "but Caserta was one of the most beautiful palaces on the planet. Once George saw it, there was no question that he wanted to shoot there."

Despite Lucasfilm's state-of-the-art model-making and computerized set-building capabilities, the director preferred to shoot the palace on location. "We've developed the technology to create sets," he explains, "but there are some things you wouldn't want to create in the computer. The palace is an incredible piece of architecture, and to try to recreate it digitally would be a vast amount of work. So it was much easier to take advantage of some of the creations that already exist than to reproduce them digitally."

Even as Lucas was filming Natalie Portman in Italy for four days in July 1997, sets precisely modeled on parts of Reggia di Caserta were in place at Leavesden for shooting other scenes. Movie audiences are likely to have a hard time distinguishing them from the real thing. Regardless, the queen and her palace will combine for a crowning achievement in *The Phantom Menace.*

BACK TO TATOOINE
On Location – Tunisia

In tracing the roots of Luke Skywalker, the ultimate hero of the original *Star Wars* trilogy, Episode I *The Phantom Menace* returns to the place Luke was raised, the desert planet Tatooine. As fate would have it, that also is where the lives of Anakin Skywalker and Obi-Wan Kenobi first intersect, setting up a series of crucial events which eventually will have a dramatic impact on the future of the galaxy.

To film the Tatooine scenes—this time they take place in and around the town of Mos Espa—Lucasfilm ventured once again to the deserts of Tunisia, a country in north Africa. The cast and crew went back to many of the same sites where parts of *A New Hope* were filmed, including the valley where R2-D2 gets zapped by Jawas and Luke and C-3PO are attacked by Sand People, as well as the area that served as the "hive of scum and villainy," Mos Eisley, the spaceport city and home of the notorious cantina. (The Tatooine scenes in *Return of the Jedi* were shot in the deserts of Arizona.)

ON LOCATION

Weeks before Director George Lucas arrived, in late July 1997, a crew of nearly 100 people descended upon a desolate spot on the edge of the Sahara, where temperatures average 130 degrees and the nearest town, Tozeur, is 25 miles away. There they would build six sets, including the entire city of Mos Espa and portions of the Podrace sequence, as well as a series of elaborate tents to serve as a base camp for the production—stocked with bare necessities, such as first-aid stations and washing machines, plus props, costumes and set dressings. "It was not a place where you could bring Winnebagos and trailers," says Producer Rick McCallum, a seasoned veteran of remote shoots, having traveled to 30 different countries over four years while working on Lucasfilm's TV series *The Young Indiana Jones Chronicles*.

The first two days of filming in the extreme conditions went well enough, and then disaster struck. During the early evening of the third day, a fierce storm ripped through the site, packing winds of up to 120 m.p.h. and a gigantic wall of sand and torrential rains that devastated the sets. Podracer engines were destroyed and scattered, hundreds of costumes were sopped with wet sand, tents were shredded, battered droids were strewn about, plaster buildings were crumbled.

RICK McCALLUM

PRODUCER

McCallum began his career in films by helping to bring to the screen *Pennies from Heaven*, starring Steve Martin. He then went on to product *I Ought to Be in Pictures*, *Dreamchild*, *Link*, *Castaway*, *The Tidy Endings*, *Strapless*, *Heading Home* and *Dennis Potter*. But for the last nine years he's only worked with *Star Wars* creator George Lucas. Together they've collaborated on *Radioland Murders* and the highly successful *The Young Indiana Jones Chronicles* TV series. McCallum also produced the *Star Wars Trilogy Special Edition* before tackling *Star Wars: Episode I The Phantom Menace*.

RAY PARK, THE
MARTIAL ARTS
EXPERT WHO
PORTRAYS DARTH
MAUL, KEPT HIS
COOL ON THE
TUNISIA SET,
DESPITE HIS HEAVY
MAKE-UP AND
BLACK ROBES. ▶

Like relief workers salvaging a post-disaster scene, the crew arrived the next morning and immediately began rebuilding and repairing. Lucas was even able to shoot on one set that had been spared. Remarkably, within a couple of days everything was up and running again, and the production remained on schedule.

Despite that calamity, McCallum reports that the sandstorm and its aftermath actually were a high point of his Episode I experience. "In a perverse sense, the sandstorm was fun. The entire crew had to quickly pull together and improvise. The adrenaline was rushing through everybody's veins, and soon an almost military feeling overtook the set. Creature designers and cameramen worked to dig equipment out of the sand. Make-up artists and caterers worked to patch together shelter from the sun. And we didn't lose a day of shooting."

Lucas came away with a positive spin on the event, too, pointing out that more than 20 years earlier a similar storm had swept through and destroyed his Tatooine sets on the original *Star Wars*. "That film went on to spectacular success," McCallum muses, "so George figured that the devastation and destruction this time was actually a good sign."

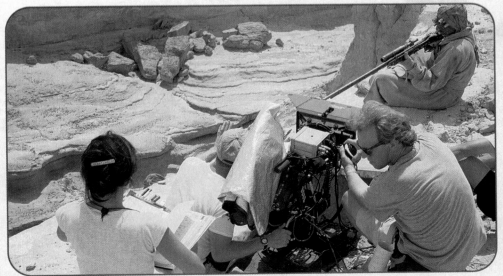

◀ LUCASFILM
RETURNED TO
SEVERAL OF THE
AREAS IN TUNISIA
WHERE THE ORIGINAL
STAR WARS WAS
FILMED, INCLUDING
THE VALLEY WHERE
LUKE SKYWALKER
WAS ATTACKED BY
SAND PEOPLE—
WHO, APPARENTLY,
HAVE ALWAYS
INHABITED THE
REGION.

Lightsabers have always been one of the most popular Star Wars™ items.
Now, these, state of the art toys come in 2 versions. Saber beams extend to over
3 feet and come with authentic movie sounds.

CAT NO. A1110 | **PRICE £49.99**

RTH MAUL CARRIES AN EVEN
LIGHTSABER

I GON JINN (Green)
ue)

CAT NO. A1111 | **PRICE £34.99**

CAT NO. A1112 | **PRICE £34.99**

100% cotton shirts are the coolest
e for a movie release. All carry 'real-life'
om the movie in fantastic and innovative
Available in Medium (M) Large (L) and X-
X). Please order by Cat No. and size

CAT NO. A9000
PRICE £10.99

CAT NO. A1060
PRICE £10.99

MONEYBANKS

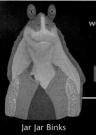

Darth Maul

2 of the coolest coin banks
we've ever seen. Could they even
make saving money fun?

CAT NO. A1049

PRICE £13.99

CAT NO. A1048

PRICE £14.99

Jar Jar Binks

EPISODE I CHESS

CAT NO. A1108 | **PRICE £34.99**

STAR WARS
CHESS SET

A fantastic Episode I chess set
featuring the major characters from the
movie, presented with a beautiful Episode
I board. Now you can relive the Episode
I battle of Light vs Dark incorporated into
our most mind-stretching game.

DARTH MAUL MASK

EVIL has a new face
in Star Wars™ Episode I and it
comes in the form of the Sith
apprentice Darth Maul. With his
horned, highly striking face, and
his double bladed lightsaber he
truly is the incarnation of
menace. This Darth Maul mask
is just one of many products to
feature Darth Mauls' image, but
the only one which transforms
you, scarily, into him.
Full head mask made from
super deluxe latex.

One size fits all.

CAT NO. A1091 | **PRICE £19.99**

LISTEN UP!

ORIGINAL MOTION PICTURE SOUNDTRACK
STAR WARS
EPISODE I
THE PHANTOM MENACE

John Williams' terrific score from Star
Wars™ Episode I

CAT NO. A6000 | **PRICE £13.99**

ME CARDS

EPISODE I: PHANTOM MENACE CHROME CARD
COLLECTORS SET
This 8 card set is the special insert set for Episode I - Phantom
Menace wide version trading cards. These cards feature the major
good and evil characters from the movie dramatically highlighted
by chromium technology. SET PRICE - £69.99

Star Wars © Lucasfilm Ltd. & TM. All Rights Reserved

TELEPHONE OR POST THE COUPON FREE OF CHARGE
TO ORDER CALL THE STAR WARS ORDER LINE ON

01621 877222

OR FAX ON 01621 850862 OR EMAIL sales@permal.demon.co.uk

**TO RECEIVE OUR FREE 32 PAGE CATALOGUE CONTAINING
HUNDREDS OF ADDITIONAL ITEMS**

CAT NO	DESCRIPTION	UNIT PRICE	QUANTITY	TOTAL
UK POSTAGE	Minimum charge £1.50, each additional item £0.50, maximum postal charge £4.50			

ORDER FORM

Please enquire
about postage
for Mainland
Europe & Rest
of World.

I enclose a cheque/postal order made payable to Sci-Fi Warehouse Direct for £ _____ | **GRAND TOTAL** £

OR debit my VISA ☐ MASTERCARD ☐ SWITCH ☐ DELTA CARD ☐ No.

☐☐☐☐ ☐☐☐☐ ☐☐☐☐ ☐☐☐☐ ☐☐☐ (Switch only)

NAME _____

ADDRESS _____

Expiry Date ☐☐ **Issue No** ☐☐ (Switch only)

Signature

POSTCODE _____ Tel: _____

SWS 799

SCI-FI WAREHOUSE DIRECT - FREEPOST, MALDON, ESSEX CM9 4XD. NORMAL DESPATCH WITHIN 14 DAYS

WE DO NOT TAKE PAYMENT until goods are ready for despatch. Please allow up to 28 days for delivery(normal delivery within 14 days),
Goods are supplied subject to availability. All videos supplied VHS only. EO&E. If you do not wish to recieve other offers please write to us.

PHANTASMIC

PHANTOM MENACE AND THE NEXT EVOLUTION OF MOVIE MAGIC

BY MARK COTTA VAZ

Imagine, in some distant future, a team of archeologists hacking through tangled overgrowth to the massive doors of a strange building. They enter and feel the rush of air, like a breath of Pharaonic oxygen escaping an Egyptian tomb. They stand stunned for a moment as they cast a light, realizing they've finally found the lost archives of the *Star Wars* empire. It would be a wonder seeing the physical artifacts—to touch the full-size landspeeder prop in which Luke seemed to skim across the Tatooine desert, to hold in their hands Imperial walkers that once trudged across the icy plains of Hoth. They'd probably see sheets of glass with painted images of the dreaded Death Star and Bespin's floating Cloud City. They might meet Yoda himself, an inscrutable smile on the old Jedi's crumbling latex face. Then they'd search every chamber until they found the evidence of the Next Evolution, that Holy of Holies—the sacred software of *Star Wars*: Episode I *The Phantom Menace*, containing all the secrets of the universe.

Time itself will judge if this sci-fi scenario proved a barrier to deeper explorations of the galaxy. By the time Luke, Leia, Han and the droids were toasting a final Rebel victory in the forest of Endor at the end of *Return of the Jedi*, Industrial Light & Magic had maxed out on the distance it could cover on the wings of traditional visual effects. Despite the fervent wishes of a planet full of *Star Wars* fans, George Lucas decided not to return to his universe until creative tools could bring to the screen unbounded visions of a universe as endless as his imagination.

▲ ILM CREATED THEED, THE EXOTIC CAPITAL OF NABOO, BY COMBINING MINIATURE MODELS OF BUILDINGS, DIGITALLY PAINTED BACKGROUNDS AND CG AND LIVE-ACTION CHARACTERS.

MODEL PROJECT SUPERVISOR CHARLIE BAILEY AND CAROLEEN GREEN PUT FINISHING TOUCHES ON PART OF THE THEED MODEL.
▼

▲ ILM BEGAN MAKING REALISTIC-LOOKING
CREATURES, LIKE THIS BEAST FROM THE DEPTHS
OF NABOO, IN *JURASSIC PARK*.

PHANTOM BREAKTHROUGHS

Flash forward to the 1990s, the decade when fantastic new computer hardware and software allowed ILM to make its dramatic breakthroughs into the frontier of the digital realm. It's a journey marked with movies that stand as milestones paving the way back to the *Star Wars* universe. In computer-generated (CG) creatures alone, the evolutionary leap went from the photorealistic dinosaurs in 1993's *Jurassic Park* to the creation, only several years later, of such synthetic performers as the friendly (and not-so-friendly) ghosts of *Casper* and the mighty dragon Draco of *Dragonheart*.

"I think because of things like *Dragonheart*, George realized this company and its people were ready to take on the synthetic characters he'd always envisioned for *Star Wars*," observes Episode I Animation Supervisor Rob Coleman. "In *The Phantom Menace*, we bring to life characters that don't exist, which you couldn't do as an animatronic or puppet creation because of the complex range of motion and action required."

Others at ILM readily agree. "There's this pure vision," says Dennis Muren, one of only four remaining veterans of the original *Star Wars* to work on Episode I, the others being digital matte painting department stalwart Paul Huston and model shop mainstays Lorne Peterson and Steve Gawley. "And with George not being as concerned with [the limits of] technology as we have been in the past, he was able to visualize beyond where he or any of us had ever been before."

◀ WHILE PARTS OF THE
PODRACE WERE SHOT
ON LOCATION IN
TUNISIA, ILM
PRODUCED MOST OF
THE VAST DESERT
EXPANSES OF THE RACE
COURSE IN ITS
COMPUTERS.

Episode I marks a new era in movies, with effects being more than whiz-bang trick shots—visual effects is now about telling stories. "We tried to break the rules," says David Dozoretz, a pre-visualization effects supervisor who utilized a computer to help Lucas plot sequences. "We took the traditional chronology of pre-production, production and post-production and turned it inside out."

Dozoretz headed up a unit allied with the overall concept design department which utilized computer "animatics," a pre-visualization tool for developing visual dynamics. Animatics once meant video cameras shooting storyboards. With computer pre-visualization, artists began plotting out sequences using 3D wire-frame figures. But with Phantom, Dozoretz and his small unit (some eight artists) took images and sequences developed by the Art Department and produced CG figures and environments with all the textures, color and motion of a high-end, commercial video game.

Dozoretz, who came onto the production in September 1995, estimates that 80% of the movie used animatics, particularly for such major sequences as the Podrace and the final battles. "There are shots in the movie identical to the animatics, with ILM's perfection applied," Dozoretz adds. "Other sequences are very different, depending on what George wanted to do."

The production uses every technique to create environments for places never seen, notably Naboo. Its exotic capital city Theed was created—beyond the on-location filming in Italy—as elaborately crafted miniature physical buildings embellished with digitally painted backgrounds and populated with CG and live-action characters. Visions of the underwater city of Otoh Gunga *(concept art above, right)*, home of the amphibious Gungan species, features many entirely CG or processed scenes.

The film is a landmark for truly ushering in the "digital backlot," that virtual production model in which live and digital actors are placed into completely synthetic, three-dimensional environments. There have been no creative shortcuts: The high-voltage Podrace in the Tatooine desert is a stunning, 10-minute sequence featuring an entire, sun-blasted expanse of sand and alien rock formations constructed as a photorealistic environment of CG, with model-shop environments and digital paintings helping to fill out the virtual landscape.

The *Phantom Menace* also provides the most ambitious interplay ever attempted between live actors and what Lucas calls his "digital actors." The digital cast is ambitious, with four starring characters and some 60 additional CG cast members appearing throughout 800 character animation shots. The main digital character, Jar Jar Binks, is a movie unto himself, appearing in some 350 shots. To

PAUL MARTIN SMITH

EDITOR

Film editor Smith brings world travel to his contribution to *The Phantom Menace*. He spent time in Canada, the United States and Europe before studying photography in Washington, D.C. He broke into the film business as an assistant cameraman on documentary films, and edited many episodes of *The Young Indiana Jones Chronicles* TV series. In addition to Episode I, Smith has worked as editor on the feature films *The Matchmaker*, *Born American* and *Edge of Innocence*.

complicate things further, the digital actors not only represent a range of physical characteristics—floppy ears, bare skin, fur—each is costumed from their own digital wardrobe, a breakthrough for ILM.

To achieve its ambitious vision, ILM needed nearly 2,000 visual effects. "There are only 10 or 15 minutes without effects in the entire movie," Muren marvels. "When George first said there'd be 2,000 shots, I thought we'd end up with maybe 800 or 1,000. But it didn't cut down!" (To put the Herculean task in perspective, consider that a huge slate of 200 visual effects shots were required to realize the off-world visions of the 1998 asteroid-disaster film *Armageddon*, and less than 500 were done for *Titanic*.)

▲ MAKING THE LIFE-LIKE SKIN, EARS, CLOTHING AND OTHER CHARACTERISTICS OF CG CHARACTERS REQUIRED ANIMATION SOFTWARE DEVELOPED SPECIFICALLY FOR EPISODE I BY ILM.

◄ COMPUTER GRAPHICS SUPERVISOR HABIB ZARGARPOUR WORKS OUT A PODRACE CRASH.

"On every show there are one or two examples of something we haven't done before, but on this there were like two dozen," says John Knoll, who shared visual effects supervisory duties with Muren and Scott Squires. "For example, there were storyboards for the climactic field battle between armies of Federation droids and Gungans that was going to be like doing *Braveheart* with computer graphics. On *The Lost World*, we had about 30 CG 'compy' [compsognathus] dinosaurs in a scene, and those shots brought our system to its knees. Now we were looking at storyboards that indicated thousands of CG characters!"

To handle the equivalent of 10 major effects productions rolled into one required special organization. The vision flowed from George Lucas, directing for the first time since *A New Hope*, while Producer Rick McCallum oversaw the entire production. The starting point for ILM would be Doug Chiang's Art Department, which translated Lucas' script into the visual foundation of concept paintings and storyboard art.

ILM's *Phantom* crew was divided into three units, one each headed by supervisors Knoll, Muren and Squires. Lucas reportedly knew it'd take more than one visual effects supervisor to helm the vast effects campaign, and particularly wanted Muren and Knoll to kick things off. With Muren wrapping up his supervisory duties on *The Lost World*, Knoll got the nod from McCallum to be on the show from the start of principal photography in England in the summer of 1997. Knoll, whose recent ILM credits included *Mission: Impossible* and work on the *Star Wars Trilogy Special Edition*, got his pick of sequences as first on board, selecting the Podrace and the dramatic space battle near the end of the film. The Knoll unit ultimately carried the brunt of the load, producing around 1,030 shots.

Muren, an eight-time Oscar winner, claimed the creation of Naboo's underwater world and the crucial battle of Gungans versus droids. Squires, who supervised Draco's creation for *Dragonheart* (earning an Academy Award nomination for Best Visual Effects), led a unit that built many of the fantastic environments of Naboo.

Other key creators, whose work encompassed all three units, included Animation Director Rob Coleman, who coordinated the work of 45 animators. Lead computer-graphics supervisor Kevin Rafferty and his team of eight CG supervisors and 78 technical directors expanded and enhanced the traditional production "pipeline," which is basically all the software tools and processing power that ILMers tap into to do their work.

The pipeline phase practically lasted the length of the production, with separate pipelines being built for a flow of software and rendering power and creative personnel to meet specific challenges, from creating all-virtual environments to putting those thousands of CG characters on screen. It was, Rafferty admits, a daunting challenge at the outset. "Wading through sheer panic, basically," Rafferty says with a laugh. "There were a lot of deer eyes in the headlights, but the feeling was, 'Let's stay the course and take one thing at a time.'"

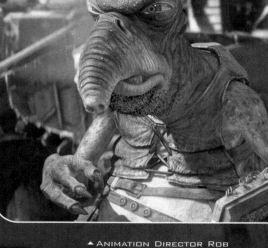

▲ ANIMATION DIRECTOR ROB COLEMAN STUDIED FILM OF ALEC GUINNESS PLAYING FAGIN IN *OLIVER* AS A BASIS FOR CREATING WATTO.

THE GALACTIC SENATE AND LIGHTSABER DUEL SCENES MERGED LIVE-ACTION BLUESCREEN SHOTS OF ACTORS WITH COMPUTER-GENERATED ELEMENTS.
▼ ▶

LAYING THE PIPELINE

In visual effects jargon, they call it a "RenderFarm," the hardware required to process and render massive amounts of digital data. For *Phantom*, ILM's RenderFarm engines featured the latest Silicon Graphics hardware, wired into 250 workstations. Yet the key to getting the job done was the development of software tools and production organization.

"We had the biggest bank of rendering engines of any show ILM has ever experienced," notes Rafferty. "Once we had artwork and storyboards, we could consider what [software tools] we already had and what we needed to develop. We had a team developing and refining the software and methodology before the crew proper came on. There were things we had to perfect, such as the CG environment for the Podrace. Our pipeline had to handle the large databases necessary for creating not only terrain, but also creatures, vehicles, dust and sky. For sequences involving the ground battle, we developed a separate pipeline and procedure by which we could put hundreds of CG creatures on screen in the same amount of time we used to show a single character."

By the time 1999 rolled around, and with the release less than a half year away, the production was humming in that creative zone where artists have the luxury of time to, as they say, "plus out" shots. "In the beginning, there was always a race going on, when we were doing a lot of parallel things, such as building the digital characters that couldn't be properly lit until they were finished," Rafferty recalls. "Once all the tools were in place, we could concentrate on keeping the ball rolling. You could put in the extra creative effort, to add an eye glint or reflections on a piece of jewelry, or make sure the virtual lighting on a CG character was working right. That's always a great place to be."

ILM AND THE FIRST UNIT

Before the arrival of digital technology, the filmmaking process was as orderly as a Victorian-era gentleman's club. There were neat divisions between the "first unit" (the "principal photography" involving actors filmed on sets or location) and "post-production," which included visual effects. Effects artists traditionally worked with the

first unit to shoot background "plates," into which separately filmed elements could be composited ("plates" evoking the earliest filmmaking era, when backgrounds were created and filmed as still photos on glass).

However, computer tools have blurred the neat distinctions, and *The Phantom Menace* practically obliterates them. Whether the Lucasfilm first unit was filming at Leavesden Studios or in the Tunisian desert, ILM maintained a constant presence—indeed, it had to. "This is the first show I've been on where I was there for everything, because there are effects in everything," says John Knoll, who regularly took a seat right next to Lucas during filming. "I'm used to being on location with the first unit to shoot plates, and typically it'll be a couple days or months. On other shows, I've not really been part of the crew, but was there to get plates and leave. This was a very different experience. I was one of the guys in the crew."

Quite apart from the completely synthetic environments, nearly all the live-action filming has subsequently been fused with visual-effects artistry: Partially built location sets were extended to dizzying heights; digitally painted landscapes were placed outside a set window where a piece of bluescreen was shot; light sources were calculated on set to make sure Jar Jar or a CG battle droid could later be added to a scene. (While the workload was tenfold, there was also a commensurate stretching of the production timetable. What Knoll estimates as the average two-to-three month period of actual production expanded on *Phantom* to 18 months.)

Knoll reports that Lucas' return to directing was a happy one. Ironically, *A New Hope*, the director's greatest success, had been emotionally and physically draining, with Lucas having to convince nervous Fox executives to stay the course, deal with problematic first-unit crews in England, get his nascent ILM effects department up and running and fight to stretch the traditional effects limits.

"George had a good time during the *Phantom* shoot," Knoll says, proving his point with an appropriate anecdote. "On the first unit, we all had to wear picture ID badges, and George had two badges made, one with a picture of Yoda and the other with Darth Vader. He said that when he was in a good mood, he'd wear the Yoda badge, but if he had the Darth Vader badge on, it would be a sign to everybody to 'beware!' Well, I never saw him wear the Vader badge."

POST PRODUCTION

◄ DENNIS MUREN'S ILM CREW UTILIZED "LIBRARIES" OF COMPUTER-ANIMATED DROIDS, SET AGAINST CG TERRAIN AND PHOTOS OF GRASSY PLAINS, IN THE EPIC GROUND BATTLE ON NABOO.

BATTLE DROID, FROM SKETCH TO MODEL TO CG. ►

PHANTOM CHARACTERS

Dennis Muren recalls the day he and Animation Supervisor Coleman were listening to Lucas describe the Gungan's underwater culture. For instance, the amphibious species' favored weapon is an energy sphere, they mine a strange goo for their power source, live in huge watertight spheres and travel the depths in submarines.

"Rob and I were thinking, 'Is he making this up, or is it what's really going on?'" Muren says. "It was half and half. These worlds, these races, are thought out individually. George is into anthropology, where your mindset is based on where you are. He gets into the details of that, of a back story that's true to itself. There's a reason the characters look and behave the way they do, why their houses look the way they do, why their weapons work the way they do. After you've worked on it for a while, you understand what that world is and that everything is rooted in a history that he [Lucas] knows and we learn."

Muren refers back to his earlier collaboration with Lucas. "He wanted characters like Yoda and Jabba to move a certain way. But he had to make compromises, because he couldn't achieve what was in his mind with latex, puppetry and animatronics. He admits there was some frustration, because he was tied down with wires and cables, and just the logistics of bringing those creatures to life. Of course, with computer graphics, we don't have to worry about the constraints of gravity and cables. CG creatures can be lit like they're 100% in the set and are able to act and interact with live actors."

Coleman grew up being wowed by movies that fused the worlds of live action and animation, memorably the fanciful sights of *Mary Poppins*, which included actor Dick Van Dyke dancing with cartoon penguins. On *Phantom*, he supervised the ultimate marriage of disparate worlds, with digital actors interacting with human performers.

Before a CG character can be imbued with the illusion of life, though, there's a long creative journey to produce the final, moveable, 3D figure. As noted, Lucas' back story was integral in the design of characters with specific personality. Through pre-production sketches and paintings, the Art Department then worked toward a character's final physical look. The transition phase from concept art to the digital realm also had to be clear on the technological and artistic capacity for animating the final 3D figure and how far to push creative boundaries.

A physical sculpture was an important step before the ILM crew headed by Geoff Campbell began constructing CG models. In some effects houses, such sculpture is scanned into the computer, but at ILM it's usually a reference. The company had learned from creating Draco and other virtual characters how much data it takes to have a CG creation look realistic when enlarged from the computer screen to the big screen without cracking the pipeline or crashing rendering systems.

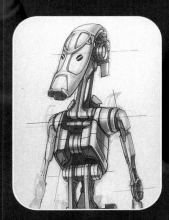

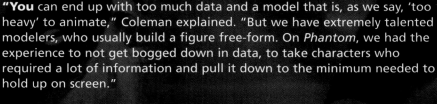

"**You** can end up with too much data and a model that is, as we say, 'too heavy' to animate," Coleman explained. "But we have extremely talented modelers, who usually build a figure free-form. On *Phantom*, we had the experience to not get bogged down in data, to take characters who required a lot of information and pull it down to the minimum needed to hold up on screen."

The bare model shells built in the computer could then be passed to Coleman and his animation team. The unit not only added flexible CG skeletons to the 3D shells, but used software to breathe into each figure the life-giving properties an animator needed to animate a character. "When you move, there's a bunching and folding of skin and muscle we call 'enveloping,' a sophisticated hardware/software and brute-force human interaction that allows a CG figure to remain true to its form, and not restrict modelers," Coleman explains. "Once the envelope was sophisticated enough, I could start assigning shots to my animators."

While actual animation ran through the popular commercial SoftImage software, the fine control over the figures required a magic lamp full of proprietary software, developed in-house at ILM, to solve the creative challenges of past shows. An example is Caricature, "an amazing software we started on *Casper*," Coleman says. "But it became really viable on *Dragonheart*, because no software in the world could provide the subtlety and control we required for the facial animation [on Draco]. We've kept updating it, so it's much more sophisticated."

The upgrading of Caricature for Episode I includes a link into another proprietary system, "physically based animation" software that features new "cloth simulation" software. The cloth software allows digital clothing to not only look realistic, but realistically move with digital bone, muscle and skin, which means that in addition to traditional "key frame" animation, animators can literally let the computer take over. "Sometimes the animation is automated, meaning clothing automatically follows the body movements, and some is simulated, meaning the software takes over and a physics and mathematical process calculates how a cut of cloth might fall or where a wrinkle can go," Coleman says. "Little bits of all those ways of getting movement can come together on a single shot."

LIGHT SOURCES HAD TO BE CAREFULLY CALCULATED AND DOCUMENTED DURING LIVE-ACTION FILMING IN ORDER TO SEAMLESSLY ADD CG ELEMENTS DURING POST-PRODUCTION.

◄ ANIMATION SUPERVISOR COLEMAN (WITH HELP FROM A DESTROYER DROID MODEL?), PUTS JAR JAR INTO A SCENE.

IT'S AMAZING JUST HOW REALISTIC JAR JAR LOOKS ON FILM, TO THE POINT WHERE HIS CG HANDS ARE ABLE TO WRAP AROUND REAL OBJECTS.
▼

Actual animation plays out with the animator watching low-resolution images on the computer screen, clicking on moveable joints and points or initiating the computer's own mathematical movements. Sometimes animators utilize "motion capture," the data obtained from human performers outfitted with sensors or other devices which digitally record particular movements. Although it was used extensively for the background animation of thousands of characters in the ground battle scenes, it was rarely used for the lead animated characters.

"We needed the animators to get the special-looking performances that had to account for the weight and shape of a character," states Muren, whose droid and Gungan battle sequence was the most character-intensive sequence in the film. "If you do an alien character completely with motion-capture data, it's going to look like a human in this other shape."

Whatever the animation challenge, the human hands at the controls are always key to a shot's success. All animators, whether in traditional line drawing or computer graphics, are surrogate actors. "I cast animators much like a casting director casts actors," says Coleman. "Some people are good at quiet dialogue shots, others are excellent at action."

To Coleman, true acting is not over-the-top histrionics, but subtleties and inflections, that stillness that draws the attention of audiences to someone seemingly doing nothing at all. "To me, great acting is when an actor is listening but still in character and in the scene. I watched actor Alec Guinness and what happens to his eyes; I particularly studied *Oliver*, where Guinness plays Fagin, [to get some insights] for Watto, the little, flying junkyard dealer. I studied what Guinness did with his hands, his eyes, how he stayed in character while moving around a room. That was the kind of detail we had to pay attention to, because we had people like Liam Neeson on the screen. If our stuff wasn't up to what he was doing, then audiences aren't going to believe it.

"What's exciting is we're now at the point where we have the kind of control we need over the faces of CG characters, their bodies, the way they breathe. We can't do every little

◄ ILM INCORPORATED
NUMEROUS HOLOGRAMS,
LIKE THIS OF SIO BIBBLE,
INTO SCENES.

SENIOR DIGITAL MATTE
ARTIST YUSEI UESUGI WORKS
ON THE SEQUENCE WHERE
AMIDALA'S ROYAL STARSHIP
LANDS ON A FLOATING
HANGAR ON CORUSCANT.
▼

facial tic or special thing a human being naturally does, but we can get close. If we're observant and aware and watching, we can bring that subtlety to a CG character, give it the kind of life behind the eyes that a human being has. Real actors have thousands of years of tradition in perfecting their craft, and we animators are now trying to catch up."

BUILDING THE DIGITAL BACKLOT

The mantra for *Phantom*'s effects could be summed up thusly: "Whatever tools are right for the job." Entire environments were conjured up in CG, from the desert expanses of Tatooine for the competition to the hilly battlefield of Naboo. But the digital backlot sometimes required a melding of computer graphics and traditional, physical models from a very busy model shop.

Such a fusion of techniques produced Theed, the fantastic Naboo city built on cliffs and surrounded by forests and waterways. The effects foundation for the capital were detailed scale buildings from ILM's model shop, which evoked an ancient, classical city that was a mix of Roman, Venetian and Arabian architecture. In some dramatic establishing shots, the queen's palace was a CG model created by Louis Katz, or a digital matte painting by Brian Flora.

"The entire city of Theed was created with a combination of virtual and physical models, as well as live-action sets and digital matte paintings," says Squires. "A number of sequences take place outdoors, so there were some buildings built on the backlot in England for live-action filming, and we built and filmed a huge number of physical miniatures to blend with that live action. There was

going to be such complexity in the buildings, with elaborate ornamentation and vegetation, we decided it would be a big deal doing it as computer graphics. So the model shop created elaborate-looking miniatures which we photographed outdoors with motion-control moves, making sure our camera work matched the moves of the live-action footage. Then we extended the city with a digital matte painting."

Squires' unit also erected the Galactic Senate as an all-CG environment. The chamber, big as the interior of a domed athletic stadium, was designed with steep sides for real sky boxes, some 1,500 individual, detachable compartments each capable of holding a few delegates. Whenever a delegation addresses the Senate, each "pod," as Squires terms them, detaches from the walls and floats to the center of the cavernous chamber.

POST PRODUCTION

The first unit built and shot several real-size boxes against bluescreen, which became elements in the composition. However, Squires not only had to render most of the rest of the boxes, but also digitally add hundreds of real alien characters. Although some CG extras were used, the complexity of aliens made it quicker to shoot greenscreen elements of human extras costumed in the exotic garb of the Galactic delegates.

Another fantastic digital backlot scenario was a 20-shot Knoll unit sequence of the Queen's Royal Starship bearing Anakin and Qui-Gon to a hangar floating amidst the skyscrapers of Coruscant. The sequence echoes the twilight landing of the *Millennium Falcon* on the outdoor hangar at Cloud City. Yet while that shot for *The Empire Strikes Back* optically composited stationary, live-action camera footage of actors with a traditional, two-dimensional oil painting of the *Falcon* and the city background, the Coruscant scenes required massive, 3D structures, bright sunshine, CG flying machines and a constantly moving virtual camera.

"These shots are called digital matte paintings, because matte painters are handling them, but they're not really hand-painted," says Senior Digital Matte Artist Yusei Uesugi, who oversaw the entire sequence. "Everything was modeled and textures applied and rendered through computer-graphics software. Each building surface needed to have a unique texture with correct scale and perspective, and it was critical that the different textures all lined up correctly. I created about 15 intensely textured CG buildings and a dozen lightly textured, more generic buildings for off-in-the-distance, which I could keep recycling with minimum modifications."

◀ THIS SEQUENCE OF
PHOTOS SHOWS THE
MODEL SET-UP AND
PYROTECHNICS CREATED
FOR THE SCENE IN
WHICH ANAKIN FIRES
THE TORPEDOES
THAT DESTROY THE
DROID CONTROL SHIP.

KNOLL'S EFFECTS
UNIT CREATED THE
EPIC SPACE BATTLE,
IN WHICH SQUADRONS
OF NABOO STARFIGHTERS
DOGFIGHT WITH TRADE
FEDERATION DROID
FIGHTERS.
▼

The Digital Matte Department was vital in creating many of the splendors of the universe. As in the old days of brush-and-oil matte paintings, entire environments were produced (such as created by Uesugi, Flora, Paul Huston and Mark Sullivan), and partially built, live-action sets were "extended" to their full dimensions by artists Kurt Kaufman, Wei Zheng, Bill Mather and Caroleen Green. Although now working with the 3D tools of traditional CG artists, they brought to computer monitors the same artistic sensibility that was once brought to a glass canvas. The success of a shot such as the Coruscant sequence still depended on the artist's eye for details: the perspective and construction of buildings; the variety of CG ships flooding the air space; the play of light and shadow; the movement of the free, flying, virtual camera.

Even as work on *Phantom* heated up, the digital matte artists were still acclimating themselves with the tools. "The biggest jump for us was the moving-camera shot, but technically it's become a standard, at least for me," says Uesugi, who began incorporating 3D digital paintings and a moving camera on the *Star Wars Trilogy Special Edition*. "I'm moving the virtual camera like a director of photography."

The ultimate digital backlot sequence was the Podrace, a mini-movie at 10 minutes and 200 shots. Anakin's dramatic race features gigantic engines (likened to two 747 jet engines tethered to a cockpit), blasting at 500 m.p.h. across a 20-mile course over a treacherous desert landscape.

The Podrace was too ambitious to be simulated with miniature sets or shot entirely on location. By Knoll's estimation, the racers' speeds meant hundreds of feet of a physical model set would be passed within seconds. And there certainly wasn't a site in Tunisia, where some Tatooine sequences were shot, exotic enough to represent such course highlights as the buttes of Mushroom Mesa.

The virtual race set was composed of a CG desert expanse stretching to the far horizons, Paul Huston's 3D paintings of weird rock formations, some model-shop environments scanned into the computer and bluescreen and CG drivers in their cockpits. The major challenge was managing the massive data. Here again, the pipeline, methodology and new software tools helped carry the day. One approach was to simply be smart in managing the information-rich landscape, avoiding carrying to the far distances "super-dense geometry," as Knoll puts it. "Close to camera you need a lot of geometric detail, but far off in frame you can get a perfectly adequate-looking image with a hundredth of the geometric detail. We had software that automatically changed resolution, did the interpolation on the ground plain depending on the difference from camera.

"We did a bit of this on *Mission: Impossible*, incorporating CG terrain with live plates shot in Scotland," Knoll adds, referring to the helicopter and train-chase sequence that was a forerunner of *Phantom*'s digital backlot. "But it was such a leap to go from that to a 10-minute sequence where nearly every shot had CG terrain. In the beginning, we weren't sure if we could create a CG landscape that looked absolutely real. Would it hold up?

BATTLE SCENE

No visit to the *Star Wars* universe is complete without lightsaber duels and massive armies fighting in space and on land. Episode I climaxes in a massive battle fought both on the ground and in the space above Naboo. On a grassy plain, the Trade Federation's droids and Gungan army battle; in space, the conflict pits Naboo starfighters ships against the Trade Federation's droid fighters and control battleship. Meanwhile, in the main hangar of the Theed palace, a to-the-death lightsaber duel matches Obi-Wan and Qui-Gon against the evil Darth Maul and his deadly, double-bladed saber.

The lightsaber fight was largely played out as another digital backlot creation, a must given the warriors fight across a walkway stretching over a seemingly bottomless pit. "For that particular sequence, we shot a combination of bluescreen and a small set piece of the walkway," says Squires, whose unit handled the duel. "In some shots, we just digitally rotoscoped the figures and put them into an all-CG world. That entailed building the computer graphics to a very detailed degree and doing an accurate match move [a linking of live-action and CG camera moves] on the characters so they looked like they were truly in that environment."

Once the lightsaber duel moved into an "energy corridor," Squires' unit faced the classic challenge of extending a live-action set that was only 12 feet high. "In many cases, that's very problematic," Squires states. "Sometimes it's easier to just do an entire virtual scene, with CG characters within it, because you can do whatever you want. In this case, we were locked into what was done in the live action. We had to match their lighting, blend into their sets."

▲ ACTORS FILMED LIGHTSABER DUELS USING SABERS WITH METAL BLADES, AND THEN ILM ADDED THE GLOWS IN POST-PRODUCTION.

The ground battle sequence, helmed by Muren's crew, was set against a largely virtual landscape with thousands of battle droids and Gungans massed against each other. The animation strategy generally utilized "libraries" of animated CG character movements that could fill out the battle scenes, with hand animation for the principal droid and Gungan combatants.

The virtual battleground itself was composed of CG terrain, as well as still photographs of rolling, green hills shot in England and northern California, which were scanned and artfully blended and processed into something otherworldly. "The skies and hills aren't typical of what you'd find on Earth—because it's supposed to be an alien planet," Muren says. "The visuals over the entire movie look more otherworldly than the other films' because there are more ways to play scenes, to build sets and make them look real. The audience can become more absorbed in what's taking place."

In Knoll's unit's space battle, squadrons of Naboo starfighters dogfight droid fighters guarding the Trade Federation's control battleship. The scene was another mix of effects, from CG starfighters to an old-fashioned motion-control element of a battleship model. Elements of doomed starfighters were created as physical "pyrotechnic" models blown up and composited into the action. "The space battle has a lot of depth to it," Knoll asserts. "There's all the action in the foreground, but we also have 30 to 40 ships in the background."

The space battle contains live-action shots, too, of pilots in their cockpits, with Knoll himself in a cameo as an intrepid Naboo pilot. "I get blown up," Knoll laughs. "I'm the only pilot you actually see die."

THE NEXT EVOLUTION

It is hard to imagine how the art and technology of filmmaking would have progressed if *Star Wars* had never been made. The trilogy not only advanced traditional effects, but ushered in the computer as a potent filmmaking tool. That leap from computer-programmed camera and model moves now encompasses CG image processing, digital actors and virtual locations. Those technologies today realize the dreams of a range of productions, from *Titanic*, which included a digital ocean and CG passengers, to the fantastic realms explored in *The Phantom Menace*.

There are legends of Tibetan mystics and Hindu yogis able to conjure up mirages of exotic palaces or humanoid creatures. In our world, it's filmmakers who now possess the magical power to create images that seem as real as reality, to create digital actors and entire environments. Ultimately, the vestiges of the Machine Age that remain—celluloid and cameras and theatrical light-projection systems—will be replaced by digital cameras and projectors.

On the scale of movie milestones, *The Phantom Menace* can be appreciated as its own breakthrough, something beyond the mere introduction of specialized tools. The movie is more about a new kind of creative process, about being able to make the biggest dreams come true.

Mark Cotta Vaz is the co-author of Industrial Light & Magic: Into the Digital Realm.

JOHN KNOLL
VISUAL EFFECTS SUPERVISOR

Along with his brother, Knoll authored the Macintosh image-processing software known as Photoshop. He's been Visual Effects Supervisor on such films as *Mission: Impossible*, the *Star Wars Trilogy Special Edition* and *Star Trek: First Contact*. Knoll was also the Computer Graphics Project Designer on *The Abyss*, for which Industrial Light & Magic won its 10th Academy Award for Best Achievement in Visual Effects.

DENNIS MUREN
SENIOR VISUAL EFFECTS SUPERVISOR

Muren brings many years of experience to his position as Senior Visual Effects Supervisor at ILM. He also brings a lot of hardware with him, in the form of the eight Oscar statuettes that he's been awarded for Best Achievement in Visual Effects. The films that have won Academy Awards for him are *Jurassic Park*, *Terminator 2*, *The Abyss*, *Innerspace*, *Indiana Jones and the Temple of Doom*, *The Empire Strikes Back*, *E.T.: The Extra-Terrestrial* and *Return of the Jedi*.

SCOTT SQUIRES
VISUAL EFFECTS SUPERVISOR

As Technical Director for *Who Framed Roger Rabbit?*, Squires helped usher to the screen one of the first highly accomplished and well-received combined live-action and animated films to ever be seen. He also worked on *The Mask*, for which he received an Academy Award nomination for Best Achievement in Visual Effects. He received a second Oscar nomination for his efforts on *Dragonheart*.

ROB COLEMAN
ANIMATION SUPERVISOR

Coleman is one of the Canadian connections on the *Star Wars* team. A graduate of Concordia University in Montreal, he first hooked up with ILM to work on another Canadian's film, *The Mask*, starring Jim Carrey. Prior to that, Coleman worked on *Captain Power*, did animation for the National Film Board and created special on-air graphics for *Much Music*.

MAXIMUM *News,* MAXIMUM *Action,*

MANGA MAX

The definitive magazine charting the latest developments in one of the fastest growing entertainment genres in the world!

Dynamic and stylish artwork, ground-breaking animation and intelligent and compelling storytelling have made the Western entertainment world sit up and look East. **Manga** (Japanese Comics) and **Animé** (Japanese Animation) as well as the fast and furious Hong Kong action cinema have taken the planet by storm.

- Includes features and opinion from the industry's best-known names: Frederik Schodt (**Manga! Manga!: The World of Japanese Comics**), Helen McCarthy (**The Anime Movie Guide**), Fred Patten (Editor of the **Complete Anime Guide**).

- Packed with Interviews, Features, Reviews, News and Previews direct from the worlds of Japanese animation, comics and Asian Action movies!

- The latest on new movies, animé television shows and video, comics and related computer games!

PHANTOM SOUNDS
BY MARK COTTA VAZ

▲ AMONG THE HUNDREDS OF NEW SOUND EFFECTS BEN BURTT CREATED FOR EPISODE I WERE THOSE HEARD IN THE PODRACE. HE DIPPED INTO HIS PAST LIBRARY OF SOUNDS FOR OTHERS, SUCH AS THE LIGHTSABERS AND BLASTERS.

While growing up in Syracuse, NY, Ben Burtt liked to listen to the wind in the willows—and the electronic hum of the mad scientist's lab in *Frankenstein*. Those same horror sounds from Universal's classic monster flicks ended up in the *Flash Gordon* serials young Burtt saw and listened to and probably influenced his future as an Academy Award-winning "sound designer" for the original *Star Wars* trilogy.

Decades later, the medium remains fantastic to him, though it's not that easy to describe. While discussing the auditory effects he designed for *The Phantom Menace*, Burtt suddenly notes, "We really don't have that many words for sound."

That sense of sound's mystery and magic helped make Burtt the guru of everything heard in the *Star Wars* universe: the hum of a lightsaber; the wind across the sands of Tatooine; footsteps along a corridor of the Death Star. Even so, Burtt has added a visual component to his repertoire (his editing work includes Lucasfilm's *Young Indiana Jones Chronicles* TV series), also serving as a "picture editor" on Episode I.

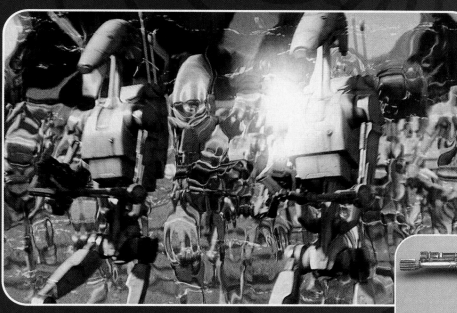

Some three years before the movie's release, Burtt, along with Editor Martin Smith, used digital "animatics" to produce low-resolution, 3D images of the universe and explore it with virtual-camera moves. Before phasing into production sound mixing, Burtt also was involved in cutting the production footage. "On this film, I've been allowed the privilege to have a filmmaker's perspective of the visual and audio flow, from picture development to the soundtrack's sound design," he observes.

His work included gauging the raw energy of the Podrace with high-intensity animatic camera angles and creating alien engine noises in the final stage of sound design and mixing. "The Podracers look like jet engines, but I've opted for popping sounds," Burtt says. "Some have high-pitched, race-car gear shifts, others are strange, synthesized motors."

In the *Star Wars* universe, every noise, except the dialogue recorded during principle photography, is fabricated. But sound still serves the story: Unlike the raw, heavily metallic acceleration of the Podracers, sounds for a conversational scene on a hangar floating amidst the spires of Coruscant had to be muted. "Here's this mega-metropolis with aerial traffic—that's what you see," says Burtt in describing the look of the ultra-modern city. "But you couldn't play up

BEN BURTT

SOUND DESIGNER

Burtt was born in Syracuse, NY, and studied physics at Allegheny College. He became part of the *Star Wars* team after being recommended as the "sound genius" who could bring to life such things as Chewbacca's "voice," which was his first of many projects. Burtt has received four Academy Awards for his sound and sound-effects work, and is also an accomplished writer and director.

POST PRODUCTION

the sound with the same visual intensity, otherwise you'd drown out the dialogue. In movies, what you do with sound is a caricature; you create something artificial."

The *Phantom Menace* echoes of the original Star Wars movies—"sound signatures" such as a lightsaber's hum or a pistol's blast mixed in with thousands of new noises—didn't extend to sound-production technology. Back on *A New Hope*, Burtt dealt with sound transferred onto 35-millimeter sprocket film. On *Phantom*, 2,500 separate sounds were digitized onto files to be managed at computer work stations.

"I'm doing the same work, but in a different manner," he asserts. "Most of the tools I used to have—a splicer, scissors, a rewind—don't exist anymore. Now we cut, paste and process sounds like someone doing word processing. The major difference is, in the past, I'd be working in a large studio with big analog machines, but now one person can have a desktop work station in the corner of a room and record, edit and mix."

Burtt keeps pictures of the old tools pasted on his computer monitor. A sleuth at tracking down sounds, the digital medium is just a new vessel in which Burtt can store anything that resonates in his eardrums.

"On a film like this, you're always on the alert for some new sound," he says. "One day I was visiting a friend's apartment, and I noticed his ceiling fan was broken, but it had an interesting buzz. I immediately recognized it as good sound for a force field. So I recorded and altered it. It became the force fields in the ground battle on Naboo."

▲ "THE PODRACERS LOOK LIKE JET ENGINES, BUT I'VE OPTED FOR POPPING SOUNDS," SAYS BEN BURTT. THE NOISES CREATED BY CLASHING LIGHTSABERS (BELOW) ARE MORE FAMILIAR.

STAR WARS ™

EPISODE I

GET THE KIT AND FEEL THE FORCE

WITH A STAR WARS AMT MODEL

30122 Anakin's Pod Racer

30118 Snap Fast Federation Starfighter

30124 Trade Federation Stap with Droid

MINI MODEL KITS

30061 Trade Federation Large Transport

30062 Republic Cruiser

30138 Trade Federation Landing Ship

30140 Sith Infiltrator

30123 Federation Tank

30130 Die Cast Naboo Starfighter
30117 Snap Fast Naboo Starfighter

AVAILABLE FROM ALL GOOD TOY STORES

AMT ERTL, THE ERTL COMPANY, FALCON ROAD, EXETER EX2 7LB
AMERANG, COMMERCE WAY, LANCING, WEST SUSSEX BN15 8TE

OUT OF THIS WORLD MODEL KITS FROM

Williams Scores Again

The Soundtrack

The music of John Williams has graced television and motion picture productions since 1953 — from *Wagon Train* to *Saving Private Ryan*. And while he has garnered more than 30 Academy Award nominations for his film scores and won five Oscars, Williams is probably best known for his *Star Wars* music, having composed, conducted and recorded the soundtracks for the original trilogy. So it is only fitting that Williams is the musical force behind Episode I *The Phantom Menace*.

In February 1999, Williams ventured to England and once again collaborated with the London Symphony Orchestra, the very same ensemble with which he recorded the first *Star Wars* film 22 years earlier. With *Phantom* Director George Lucas and Producer Rick McCallum at his side, and a rough cut of the movie for reference, Williams and the L.S.O. converged on the famous Abbey Road Studios (of Beatles fame) and came away with another masterpiece. From the familiar "*Star Wars* Main Theme"—one of the most recognized pieces of film music ever—to the dramatic "Duel of the Fates," the all-new score is a perfect accompaniment to the latest chapter in the saga.

Lucas himself best summarizes Williams' achievement in the liner notes he wrote for the *Phantom Menace* soundtrack: "Composing the score for Episode I [was] a daunting task. Gone were so many of the characters and situations that his music now indelibly evokes. In Episode I, there is no Luke Skywalker, no Princess Leia, no Han Solo, no evil Empire, and even Darth Vader is an innocent little boy. John had to draw upon the signature themes while creating a new, if somehow familiar, musical galaxy. And he had to visit new emotional territory in Episode I. His music had to help tell the story of a pacifist Queen who confronts the need to fight for the survival of her people, a mother who must give up her son so that he might achieve his true potential and noble Jedi faced with the rise of an unimaginable evil. Once again, John has exceeded my expectations and produced a lavish, rich, moving and thrilling score."

For his part, Williams was honored to continue his association with *Star Wars*, and discovered first-hand at the recording session just how deep its impression runs. "I was delighted to see that there were a dozen or so members of the orchestra who had played on the original 1977 soundtrack," the conductor writes in his contribution to the liner notes. "During our first intermission, several of the younger players approached me and explained that, as children, they had seen and heard *Star Wars*, and immediately resolved to study music with the goal of playing with the London Symphony."

The Episode I soundtrack is released by Sony Classical, on CD, cassette and mini disc. The sheet music is published by Warner Chappell. Following is a complete track list, with timings:

1	*Star Wars* **Main Title** *and* **The Arrival at Naboo**	2:55
2	**Duel of the Fates**	4:14
3	**Anakin's Theme**	3:09
4	**Jar Jar's Introduction** *and* **The Swim to Otoh Gunga**	5:07
5	**The Sith Spacecraft** *and* **The Droid Battle**	2:37
6	**The Trip to the Naboo Temple** *and* **The Audience with Boss Nass**	4:10
7	**The Arrival at Tatooine** *and* **The Flag Parade**	4:04
8	**He Is the Chosen One**	3:53
9	**Anakin Defeats Sebulba**	4:24
10	**Passage through the Planet Core**	4:40
11	**Watto's Deal** *and* **Kids at Play**	4:57
12	**Panaka and the Queen's Protectors**	3:24
13	**Queen Amidala** *and* **The Naboo Palace**	4:51
14	**The Droid Invasion** *and* **The Appearance of Darth Maul**	5:14
15	**Qui-Gon's Noble End**	3:48
16	**The High Council Meeting** *and* **Qui-Gon's Funeral**	3:09
17	**Augie's Great Municipal Band** *and* **End Credits**	9:37

JOHN WILLIAMS

MUSICAL COMPOSER

Williams already had an Oscar under his belt, for *Fiddler on the Roof*, when he was introduced to George Lucas by Steven Spielberg. Lucas was looking for someone to compose music for *Star Wars*. It turned out to be an auspicious introduction, as it would lead to Williams' third Academy Award—after picking up his second one for Spielberg's *Jaws*. Besides composing the music for all the *Star Wars* movies, Williams has served as music director for more than 75 films and has written many concert pieces, as well as the themes for the 1984, 1988 and 1996 Summer Olympic Games.

Licensed To Thrill

Star Wars merchandise has been popular with fans for the past 22 years, and the tradition continues with *The Phantom Menace*. What follows is a colorful sampling of the quality, creativity and innovation of the Episode I merchandise from several licensed manufacturers.

HASBRO HAS INCORPORATED NEW TECHNOLOGY INTO ITS 3 3/4" ACTION FIGURES, CALLED COMMTECH, WHICH ENABLES QUI-GON, R2-D2, C-3PO AND OTHER CHARACTERS TO "SPEAK" KEY LINES FROM THE MOVIE. ALAN HASSENFELD, HASBRO'S CHAIRMAN AND CEO, DUBBED COMMTECH THE "DIGITAL TRADING CARD FOR THE NEXT MILLENNIUM." (*COMMTECH READER* SHOWN IN INSET PHOTO.) HASBRO WILL RELEASE MORE THAN 35 ACTION FIGURES, PLUS VEHICLES AND COLLECTOR DOLLS, IN A VARIETY OF FORMATS AND PRICE POINTS.

APPLAUSE HAS A WIDE RANGE OF *PHANTOM MENACE* GIFT ITEMS, FROM PVC FIGURES, KEYCHAINS AND MAGNETS TO LIGHT-UP MEGA COLLECTIBLES—LARGE, VINYL DOLLS SOLD IN GORGEOUS WINDOW-BOX PACKAGING. ALSO LOOK FOR EXQUISITE FIGURAL HEADS, SUCH AS THIS ONE OF THE TREACHEROUS DARTH MAUL. "MOST OF OUR PIECES FEATURE HAND-CRAFTED ELEMENTS. SOME ARE ENTIRELY HAND-CAST, HAND-PAINTED AND HAND-POLISHED," REMARKS CHAZ FITZHUGH, APPLAUSE'S DIRECTOR OF BRAND MANAGEMENT.

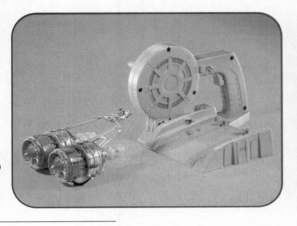

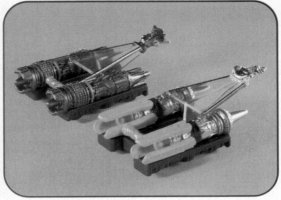

GALOOB TOYS, A SUBSIDIARY OF HASBRO, IS PRODUCING DOZENS OF EPISODE I TOYS, INCLUDING 10 MICRO MACHINES COLLECTIONS OF MINI VEHICLES AND FIGURES, DIE-CAST TOYS, PLAYSETS AND LARGER ACTION FLEET VEHICLE COLLECTIONS. BRAND NEW IS A MICRO MACHINES LINE CALLED PODRACING, WHICH ALLOWS FANS TO BUILD THEIR OWN PODRACERS. ESPECIALLY CLEVER ARE THE MINIATURE FIGURE HEADS THAT OPEN TO REVEAL TINY FIGURES AND MOVIE SCENES.

LEGO SYSTEMS ADDED *STAR WARS* TO ITS PRODUCT MIX IN 1999—MARKING THE COMPANY'S FIRST FORAY INTO THE LICENSING WORLD. FOLLOWING AN INITIAL LINE OF "CLASSIC" TOYS BASED ON THE ORIGINAL FILM TRILOGY, LEGO HAS RELEASED EIGHT DIFFERENT EPISODE I VEHICLE BUILDING SETS, SUCH AS THIS PODRACING SET. EACH COMES WITH CUTE LITTLE LEGO VERSIONS OF KEY *PHANTOM MENACE* CHARACTERS. ARRIVING LATER WILL BE MINDSTORMS DROID DEVELOPER KITS, WITH WHICH YOU CAN BUILD YOUR OWN DROID, INCLUDING A BATTLE DROID OR R2-D2. THE DROIDS CAN BE PROGRAMMED TO DO YOUR BIDDING THROUGH A SO-CALLED RCX BRICK CHIP. "LEGO PLAY MATERIALS STIMULATE CHILDREN'S IMAGINATION, CREATIVITY AND PERSONAL DEVELOPMENT," SAYS PETER EIO, PRESIDENT OF LEGO. "*STAR WARS* MIRRORS MANY OF THE SAME VALUES AS OUR TOYS, IN THAT IT IS A TIMELESS EPIC SAGA, ENJOYED BY GENERATIONS, WHICH CELEBRATES THE QUALITIES OF COURAGE, HEROISM AND FRIENDSHIP THROUGH A VERY IMAGINATIVE AND EXCITING STORY."

MERCHANDISE

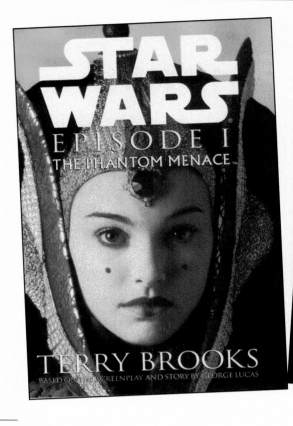

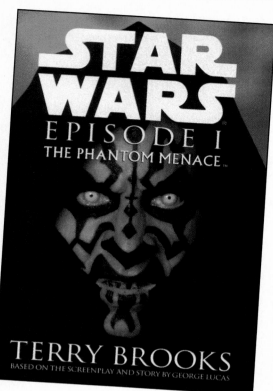

THE FIRST WORD IN EPISODE I BOOK TIE-INS IS BALLANTINE, WHICH HAS SEVERAL TITLES IN STORE FROM ITS DEL REY IMPRINT, BEGINNING WITH *THE PHANTOM MENACE* HARDCOVER NOVELIZATION, WRITTEN BY TERRY BROOKS,
THE BEST-SELLING AUTHOR OF THE *SWORD OF SHANNARA* FANTASY SERIES. QUADRUPLING INTEREST WILL BE FOUR VARIATIONS OF THE COVER. *THE MAKING OF STAR WARS: EPISODE I THE PHANTOM MENACE* FEATURES INTERVIEWS WITH GEORGE LUCAS AND KEY CAST AND CREW MEMBERS, AS WELL AS FASCINATING BEHIND-THE-SCENES ARTICLES. *STAR WARS: EPISODE I THE ILLUSTRATED SCREENPLAY*, WRITTEN BY LUCAS HIMSELF, CONTAINS NEARLY 250 STORYBOARDS, THE BULK OF WHICH WERE SKETCHED BY DESIGN DIRECTOR DOUG CHIANG. *THE ART OF THE PHANTOM MENACE*, DUE OUT IN LATE '99, IS A HARDCOVER, COFFEE-TABLE BOOK FEATURING CHIANG'S FULL-COLOR PRODUCTION PAINTINGS.

CHANGES WILL RELEASE BETWEEN 60 AND 70 EPISODE I T-SHIRTS, IN GIFT, SPECIALTY AND DEPARTMENT STORES. THE APPAREL MAKER HAS GONE BEYOND JUST SCREEN-PRINTING ON BASIC T'S: THE LINE INCLUDES SUCH INNOVATIONS AS GLOW-IN-THE-DARK AND METALLIC INKS AND FLOCK PRINTING. SHIRT STYLES INCLUDE JUNIOR FASHION AND TANK TOPS. CHANGES' TEAM OF 32 CREATIVE DESIGNERS DEVELOPED THE COLORFUL LINE.

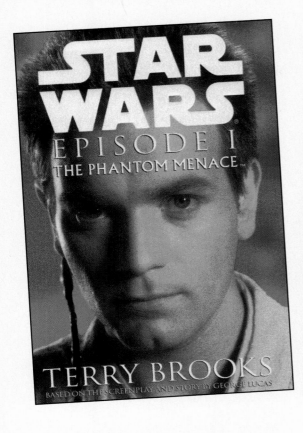

THE TOPPS COMPANY is celebrating its 22-year relationship with Lucasfilm with its first series of Episode I trading cards. Produced in its groundbreaking, UV-coated, Widevision format, the cards capture movie images directly from the film. There are 80 cards in the mass-market version, while the hobby edition contains 120 different cards (call 888 comic book to locate the nearest retailer carrying this version). "Our Star Wars trading cards are considered the gold standard in the entertainment-card category, because they embody many of the same qualities of the movies themselves: fun, cutting-edge technology and interactivity," says Ira Friedman, Vice President, Publishing and New Product Development for Topps. "Episode I, with all its spectacular imagery and story depth, provides us with a wonderful opportunity to continue delivering fans and collectors with the very best in Star Wars trading cards."

MERCHANDISE

DECIPHER HAS DEVELOPED SEVERAL EPISODE I COLLECTIBLE TRADING CARD GAME SETS. SIXTY-CARD STARTER DECKS (WITH INSTRUCTIONS ON HOW TO PLAY) AND 11 CARD EXPANSION PACKS CONTAINING COMMON, UNCOMMON AND RARE CARDS MAKE UP EACH 130-CARD SET. EXPANSION SETS INCLUDE "MENACE OF DARTH MAUL," "THE JEDI COUNCIL" AND "BATTLE OF NABOO."

THE THREE MOST POPULAR VIDEO GAME PLATFORMS—3D ACCELERATED PC, NINTENDO 64 AND SONY PLAYSTATION—HAVE EPISODE I GAMES BASED ON A CERTAIN NEW ADVENTURE MOVIE, ALL DEVELOPED BY LUCASARTS ENTERTAINMENT. EPISODE I: RACER IS NOT ONLY THE FIRST STAR WARS RACING GAME EVER, BUT THE FIRST OF ITS TYPE FROM LUCASARTS. DESIGNED FOR NINTENDO 64 AND 3D ACCELERATED PC SYSTEMS, THE GAME TAKES A SHORT, BUT VERY INTENSE SCENE FROM THE FILM AND TURNS IT INTO A FULL-THROTTLE GAMING EXPERIENCE. AMONG ENVIRONMENTS WHERE PLAYERS TRAVEL ARE AN ASTEROID PLANET, AN ICE PLANET AND TATOOINE. SOME LEVELS ARE BASED ON THE MOVIE, WHILE OTHERS ARE COMPLETELY ORIGINAL. BUT SUCH FAMILIAR STAR WARS ELEMENTS AS DROIDS AND SANDCRAWLERS SHOULD MAKE EVERY FAN FEEL RIGHT AT HOME.

NEW FOR 99

Your favourite Star Wars character is now available in useable plush

STAR WARS™
EPISODE I

Visit your nearest stockist or for further information contact us direct on: Tel (01908) 288100

THE RANGE

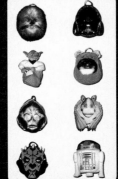

Chewbacca Rucksack	Darth Vader Rucksack
Chewbacca Purse	Darth Vader Rucksack (Med)
Chewbacca Bumbag	Darth Vader Purse
Chewbacca Plush Magnet	Darth Vader Plush Magnet
Chewbacca Resin Magnet	Darth Vader Resin Magnet
Yoda Rucksack	Ewok Wicket Shoulder Bag
Yoda Plush Magnet	Ewok Wicket Plush Magnet
C3PO Rucksack	Jar Jar Binks Rucksack
C3PO Bumbag	Jar Jar Binks Purse
C3PO Purse	Jar Jar Binks Bumbag
C3PO Resin Magnet	Jar Jar Binks Plush Magnet
Darth Maul Rucksack	R2D2 Rucksack
Darth Maul Bumbag	R2D2 Rucksack (Med)
Darth Maul Plush Magnet	R2D2 Purse
Darth Maul Resin Magnet	

MORE EPISODE 1 CHARACTERS TO FOLLOW

GIFTWARE INTERNATIONAL PLC,
THE GIFT WAREHOUSE,
2 NEWMARKET COURT,
CHIPPENHAM DRIVE, KINGSTON,
MILTON KEYNES, MK10 0AQ

TEL: +44 (0) 1908 288100
FAX: +44 (0) 1908 288109
EMAIL: giftplc@aol.com

STARTS HERE!

STAR WARS COMIC

As seen on TV, the UK's only official magazine entirely dedicated to the very best official **Star Wars** comic strip adventures. Features the comic strip adaptation of *Star Wars: Episode I The Phantom Menace* and a special prequel strip, detailing the backstory to the new film.

The first issue of the **Star Wars Comic** goes on sale 12 July 1999 for two weeks. It will be available weekly from the second issue. This is a must for **Star Wars** fans and collectors everywhere.
ONLY £1.25

STAR WARS EPISODE I OFFICIAL SOUVENIR EDITION

Titan Magazines is proud to present the Official Souvenir Edition for the film that starts it all. This full-colour magazine includes exclusive interviews with the on-screen and behind-the-scenes stars. This 116-page, squared-bound, full-colour throughout magazine goes on sale 25 June.

Plus: behind-the-scenes features on the stunning special effects and exotic locations. This is the must-have guide to Episode I!
ONLY £4.99

STAR WARS POSTER MAGAZINES

ISSUE 1 *HEROES* ON SALE 2 JULY
ISSUE 2 *VILLAINS* ON SALE 23 JULY
Titan will bring *Star Wars: Episode I The Phantom Menace* to the walls of bedrooms everywhere with this pair of official, 24-page poster magazines. The format of each poster magazine is a deluxe 8-page double gatefold "pin-up cover" backed with a locker poster; plus a 16-page fold-out jumbo poster backed with cool photos, art and text, including pin-ups, character profiles and descriptions of weapons, vehicles and spaceships.
ONLY £2.50
FOLDS OUT INTO GIANT
FULL-COLOUR POSTER!

STAR WARS MAGAZINE

Star Wars Magazine has all the latest official news, features, photos, interviews, competitions and updates from the new film as well as the original trilogy. Forget the rest, pick up the best! As *Star Wars: Episode I The Phantom Menace* premieres, **Star Wars Magazine** continues to report on the film's journey to our screens. Available every two months from all good newsagents and specialist stores.
ONLY £3.25

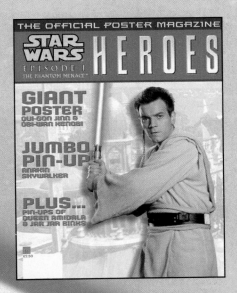

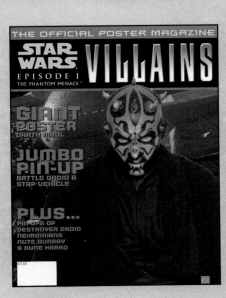

EVERY SAGA HAS A BEGINNING

STAR WARS
EPISODE I
THE PHANTOM MENACE

STAR WARS EPISODE I THE PHANTOM MENACE
Starring LIAM NEESON EWAN McGREGOR NATALIE PORTMAN JAKE LLOYD IAN McDIARMID
Co-starring ANTHONY DANIELS KENNY BAKER PERNILLA AUGUST FRANK OZ
Music by JOHN WILLIAMS Produced by RICK McCALLUM
Written and Directed by
GEORGE LUCAS

   Special Visual Effects and Animation by INDUSTRIAL LIGHT & MAGIC
A LUCASFILM LTD. Production – A TWENTIETH CENTURY FOX Release
Soundtrack Available on SONY CLASSICAL Read the Novel from DEL REY BOOKS
W W W . S T A R W A R S . C O M

SEE and READ THE FILM ...

The graphic novel tie-in to *Star Wars: Episode I The Phantom Menace* is available now as a full colour paperback. Adapted from George Lucas' original screenplay *Star Wars: Episode I The Phantom Menace* unlocks the history and events that laid the foundation for the Rebel Alliance's epic struggle against the Empire as chronicled in the original **Star Wars** film trilogy. Full colour comic strip.

£9.99

FEAR IS THE PATH TO THE DARK SIDE... FEAR LEADS TO ANGER... ANGER LEADS TO HATE... HATE LEADS TO SUFFERING.

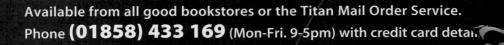

CREDITS

WRITTEN & DIRECTED BY GEORGE LUCAS

PRODUCED BY RICK McCALLUM

EXECUTIVE PRODUCER	GEORGE LUCAS
DIRECTOR OF PHOTOGRAPHY	DAVID TATTERSALL, B.S.C.
PRODUCTION DESIGNER	GAVIN BOCQUET
EDITED BY PAUL MARTIN SMITH G.B.F.E., BEN BURTT	
COSTUME DESIGNER	TRISHA BIGGAR
CASTING BY ROBIN GURLAND	
MUSIC BY JOHN WILLIAMS	

STARRING
LIAM NEESON
EWAN McGREGOR
NATALIE PORTMAN
JAKE LLOYD
PERNILLA AUGUST
AND FRANK OZ AS YODA

CO-STARRING
IAN McDIARMID   OLIVER FORD DAVIES   HUGH QUARSHIE
AHMED BEST   ANTHONY DANIELS   KENNY BAKER
WITH TERENCE STAMP AS CHANCELLOR VALORUM

DESIGN DIRECTOR	DOUG CHIANG
VISUAL EFFECTS SUPERVISORS	
JOHN KNOLL DENNIS MUREN	SCOTT SQUIRES
ANIMATION DIRECTOR	ROB COLEMAN
PRODUCTION SUPERVISOR	DAVID BROWN
LIVE-ACTION CREATURE EFFECTS SUPERVISOR	NICK DUDMAN
CHIEF MAKE-UP ARTIST	PAUL ENGELEN
FIRST ASSISTANT DIRECTOR	CHRIS NEWMAN
SECOND ASSISTANT DIRECTOR	BERNARD BELLEW
THIRD ASSISTANT DIRECTOR	BEN HOWARTH

CAST

QUI-GON JINN	LIAM NEESON
OBI-WAN KENOBI	EWAN McGREGOR
QUEEN AMIDALA/PADMÉ	NATALIE PORTMAN
ANAKIN SKYWALKER	JAKE LLOYD
SENATOR PALPATINE	IAN McDIARMID
SHMI SKYWALKER	PERNILLA AUGUST
SIO BIBBLE	OLIVER FORD DAVIES
CAPTAIN PANAKA	HUGH QUARSHIE
JAR JAR BINKS	AHMED BEST
C-3PO	ANTHONY DANIELS
R2-D2	KENNY BAKER
YODA	FRANK OZ
CHANCELLOR VALORUM	TERENCE STAMP
BOSS NASS	BRIAN BLESSED
WATTO	ANDREW SECOMBE
DARTH MAUL	RAY PARK
SEBULBA	LEWIS MACLEOD
WALD	WARWICK DAVIS
CAPTAIN TARPALS	STEVEN SPEIRS
NUTE GUNRAY	SILAS CARSON
RUNE HAAKO	JEROME BLAKE
DAULTAY DOFINE	ALAN RUSCOE
RIC OLIÉ	RALPH BROWN
FIGHTER PILOT BRAVO 5	CELIA IMRIE
FIGHTER PILOT BRAVO 2	BENEDICT TAYLOR
FIGHTER PILOT BRAVO 3	CLARENCE SMITH
MACE WINDU	SAMUEL L. JACKSON
PALACE GUARD	DOMINIC WEST
RABÉ	CRISTINA da SILVA
EIRTAÉ	FRIDAY (LIZ) WILSON
YANÉ	CANDICE ORWELL
SACHÉ	SOFIA COPPOLA
SABÉ	KIERA KNIGHTLEY
REPUBLIC CRUISER CAPTAIN	BRONAGH GALLAGHER
REPUBLIC CRUISER PILOT	SILAS CARSON
TC-14	JOHN FENSOM
FODÉ	GREG PROOPS
BEED	SCOTT CAPURRO
JABBA THE HUTT	HIMSELF
JIRA	MARGARET TOWNER
KITSTER	DHRUV CHANCHANI
SEEK	OLIVER WALPOLE
AMEE	JENNA GREEN
MELEE	MEGAN UDALL
EETH KOTH	HASSANI SHAPI
ADI GALLIA	GIN
SAESEE TIIN	KHAN BONFILS
YARAEL POOF	MICHELLE TAYLOR
EVEN PIELL	MICHAELA COTTRELL
DEPA BILLABA	DIPIKA O'NEILL JOTI
YADDLE	PHIL EASON

AKS MOE	MARK COULIER
YODA PUPPETEERS	KATHY SMEE
	DON AUSTEN
	DAVID GREENAWAY
VOICE OF TC-14	LINDSAY DUNCAN
VOICE OF DARTH MAUL	PETER SERAFINOWICZ
VOICE OF RUNE HAAKO	JAMES TAYLOR
VOICE OF DAULTAY DOFINE	CHRIS SANDERS
VOICE OF LOTT DOD	TOBY LONGWORTH
VOICE OF AKS MOE	MARC SILK
VOICE OF TEY HOW	TYGER

STUNT COORDINATOR/SWORDMASTER	NICK GILLARD
ASST STUNT COORDINATOR/OBI-WAN DOUBLE	ANDREAS PETRIDES
STUNT PERFORMER/QUI-GON DOUBLE	ROB INCH

STUNT PERFORMERS: DOMINIC PREECE, MORGAN JOHNSON, MARK NEWMAN, JOSS GOWER, RAY DE-HAAN, DANNI BIERNAT

SUPERVISING ART DIRECTOR	PETER RUSSELL

ART DIRECTORS: FRED HOLE, JOHN KING, ROD McLEAN, PHIL HARVEY

ART DIRECTOR (TUNISIA)	BEN SCOTT

DRAUGHTSMEN: PAUL CROSS, NEIL MORFITT, GARY TOMKINS, TOAD TOZER, JULIE PHILPOTT, JANE CLARK PEARCE, PHILIP ELTON, MIKE BISHOP, LUCY RICHARDSON

SCENIC ARTIST	JAMES GEMMILL

UK CONCEPT ARTISTS: TONY WRIGHT, KUN CHANG

UK ART DEPARTMENT COORDINATOR	LAURA BURROWS

JUNIOR DRAUGHTSMEN: HELEN XENOPOULOS, REMO TOZZI
SCULPTORS: EDDIE BUTLER, TESSA HARRISON, RICHARD MILLS, KEITH SHORT, RICHARD SMITH
US CONCEPT ARTISTS: IAIN McCAIG, TERRYL WHITLATCH, JAY SHUSTER, ED NATIVIDAD, KURT KAUFMAN, MARC GABBANA

STORYBOARD ARTIST BENTON JEW	

CONCEPT SCULPTORS: TONY McVEY, MARK SIEGEL, RICHARD MILLER, ROBERT BARNES
CONCEPT MODEL MAKERS: JOHN GOODSON, JOHN DUNCAN, ELLEN LEE
3-D COMPUTER MODELLERS: CAINE DICKINSON, SIMON DUNSDON
US ART DEPARTMENT COORDINATORS: JILL JURKOWITZ, BLAKE TUCKER

US ART DEPARTMENT ASSISTANT	TOM BARRATT

UK ART DEPARTMENT ASSISTANTS: CHRISTOPHER CHALLONER, IAIN McFADYEN, CLAIRE NIA RICHARDS, EMMA TAUBER
CONCEPTUAL RESEARCHERS: JONATHAN BRESMAN, DAVID CRAIG, KOICHI KURISU

PRE-VISUALIZATION/EFFECTS SUPERVISOR	DAVID DOZORETZ

PRE-VISUALIZATION/EFFECTS ARTISTS: EVAN PONTORIERO, RYAN TUDHOPE, KEVIN BAILLIE, JEFF WOZNIAK

PRODUCTION MANAGER	JO BURN
PRODUCTION MANAGER (TUNISIA)	PETER HESLOP
UNIT MANAGER (TUNISIA)	JEREMY JOHNS
SCRIPT SUPERVISOR	JAYNE-ANN TENGGREN
ASSISTANT TO RICK McCALLUM (UK)	ISOBEL THOMAS

ASSISTANTS TO RICK McCALLUM (US): JANET NIELSEN, SOPHIE MILTON

EXECUTIVE ASSISTANT TO GEORGE LUCAS	JANE BAY
SECRETARY TO GEORGE LUCAS	ANNE MERRIFIELD

PRODUCTION COORDINATORS: LISA PARKER, HERMIONE NINNIM

PRODUCTION COORDINATOR (TUNISIA)	TORI PARRY
PRODUCTION COORDINATOR (ITALY)	WINNIE WISHART
PRODUCTION COORDINATOR (TRAVEL)	MEL CLAUS
ASSISTANT PRODUCTION COORDINATOR	LEO MARTIN
UNIT NURSE	JEANIE UDALL

LOCATION MANAGERS: ROBERT JORDAN, RICHARD SHARKEY

EXTRAS CASTING	SALLY MILLSON
CASTING ASSISTANT	KIRSTEN HAMPTON

ARTISTS' ASSISTANTS: KATE JONES, JEMMA KEARNEY

CROWD ASSISTANT DIRECTOR	PAUL HIGGINS
FLOOR RUNNERS	TAMANA BLEASDALE, NATHAN HOLMES
STUDIO RUNNERS	MELISSA LEIGH, HENRY FORSYTH, JOE HALFORD, MARC WILTON, MARTIN BROWN
PRODUCTION NETWORK ENGINEER	PAUL MATWIY
FIRE SAFETY OFFICER	DAVID DEANE

PRODUCTION CONTROLLER	KATHRYN FARRAR
PRODUCTION ACCOUNTANT	MICHELE TANDY
SET COST ACCOUNTANT	BETTY WILLIAMS
ACCOUNTING MANAGER	WENDY GORMAN
LOCATION ACCOUNTANT (TUNISIA)	DEAN HOOD
LOCATION ACCOUNTANT (ITALY)	VAL SUNDERLAND
ASSISTANT ACCOUNTANT (TUNISIA)	CLARE PLUMMER

ASSISTANT ACCOUNTANTS: RAJESHREE PATEL, PENELOPE POWELL, BARBARA HARLEY

ACCOUNTS ASSISTANT	JEAN SIMMONS

ACCOUNTS RUNNER	SARAH-JANE WHEALE
ASSISTANT TO CONTROLLER	ARDEES RABANG JUNDIS
CAMERA OPERATOR	TREVOR COOP
AERIAL CAMERAMAN	ADAM DALE
HELICOPTER PILOT	MARK WOLFE

FOCUS PULLERS: GRAHAM HALL, BEN BUTLER
CLAPPER/LOADERS: JASON COOP, SHAUN EVANS

STEADICAM OPERATOR	KEITH SEWELL
KEY GRIP	PETER MYSLOWSKI
SOUND RECORDIST	JOHN MIDGLEY
BOOM OPERATOR	JUNE PRINZ
SOUND ASSISTANT	CRAIG BURNS
LOCATION MATCHMOVE SUPERVISOR	JACK HAYE
MATCHMOVER	EDWARD COTTON

VIDEO PLAYBACK: LESTER DUNTON, ANDREW HADDOCK
VIDEO PLAYBACK ASSISTANT: DATHI SVEINBJARNARSON

EFFECTS VIDEO ENGINEER	CLARK HIGGINS
SET DECORATOR	PETER WALPOLE
ASSISTANT SET DECORATOR	AMANDA BERNSTEIN
PRODUCTION BUYER	DEBORAH STOKELY
SUPERVISING DRESSING PROPMAN	MARTIN KINGSLEY

CHARGEHAND DRESSING PROPMEN: PETER WATSON, KEITH PITT

DRESSING PROPMAN	BRIAN ALDRIDGE
PROPERTY MASTER	TY TEIGER
CHARGEHAND PROPMAKER	OLIVER HODGE
SENIOR PROPMAKER	TOBY HAWKES

PROPMAKERS: HOWARD MUNFORD, JOHN WELLER, PIERRE BOHANNA, JIM BARR, WESLEY PEPPIATT, BRUCE CHEESMAN, NICK TURNBULL, PETER LOOBY, GRANT TARBOX, TERRY TOOHILL, PAUL HEARN, MATTHEW FOSTER, SANDER ELLERS, LEE REEDER, JEFF KNIGHT

PROP STOREMAN	JONATHAN HURST

DRAPESMEN: COLIN FOX, FRANK HOWE

SUPERVISING STAND-BY PROPMAN	BERNARD HEARN
STAND-BY PROPMAN	DANIEL HEARN
ASSISTANT COSTUME DESIGNER	ANN MASKREY
WARDROBE SUPERVISOR	SHARON LONG
CROWD PRE-FIT SUPERVISOR	SARAH JANE TOUAIBI
WARDROBE MASTER	ANTHONY BROOKMAN
WARDROBE MISTRESS	LOU DURKIN

WARDROBE ASSISTANTS: HELEN MATTOCKS, NEIL MURPHY, NATALIE RODGERS
COSTUME PAINTERS: JOHN COWELL, STEVEN GELL
TEXTILE ASSISTANTS: MARTIN McSHANE, EMMA WALKER
COSTUME PROPS ASSISTANTS: REUBEN HART, PETER THOMPSON
COSTUME ACCESSORIES: KAREN SHANNON, EMMA FRYER
COSTUME RUNNERS: KARN WEBSTER, AMBER SMIT

COSTUME WORKROOM SUPERVISOR	NICOLE YOUNG
COSTUME ASSISTANT	MICHAEL MOONEY

CUTTERS: KAY COVENEY, SHARON McCORMACK, DEBBIE MARCHANT

COSTUME PROPS MODELLER	IVO COVENEY

WORKROOM ASSISTANTS: ANNE MATHESON, MARNIE ORMISTON, ARABELLA DEAN, ROSLYN TIDDY, ANGELA CREASOR, JULIE NETHERCOAT, RACHEL TURNER, RUTH MATHESON, ANDREA MOON, CAROLINE MIRFIN, ROSARIA COPPOLA

ARMOR MAKERS	FBFX
CONSTRUCTION MANAGER	DAVID BUBB
ASSISTANT CONSTRUCTION MANAGER	LEON APSEY
CHIEF SCAFFOLDING ENGINEER	STEVE SANSOM
H.O.D. CARPENTER	ROBERT SUTTON
H.O.D. PLASTERER	KEN BARLEY
H.O.D. PAINTER	JOHN DAVEY
H.O.D. STAGEHAND	KEITH MUIR

SUPERVISING CARPENTERS: KARL APSEY, BRIAN BLUES

SUPERVISING PLASTERER	MICHAEL GARDINER
SUPERVISING PAINTER	PAUL WHITELOCK
SUPERVISING SCENIC PAINTER	MICHAEL GUYETT
SUPERVISING WOOD MACHINIST	STEPHEN WESTON

CHARGEHAND CARPENTERS: WAYNE DAY, JIM KERR, JOHN KIRSOP, SIMON MARJORAM, TOM McCARTHY

CHARGEHAND PAINTER	DAVID CARTER

CHARGEHAND RIGGERS: PETER CONNOLLY, JOHN HARRIS, PAUL MILLS, BILL SANSOM, WOLFGANG WALTHER
CHARGEHAND PLASTERERS: ETTORE VENTURINI, STEVE COURT, PATRICK LAHO

CHARGEHAND PAINT SPRAYER	STAN LATTIMORE
STAND-BY CARPENTER	JASON PHELPS
STAND-BY RIGGER	JASON CURTIS
STAND-BY PAINTER	KEVIN McCARTHY
STAND-BY STAGEHAND	JAMES MUIR

CONSTRUCTION SECRETARIES: CHARLOTTE BIGGS, SARAH BUBB, MICHELE HUDD
CONSTRUCTION NURSES: NICKY JARVIS, MARCIA BAMGBOYE

THANKS TO ALL THE UK CONSTRUCTION CREW

CREATURE EFFECTS COORDINATOR · LYN NICHOLSON
ANIMATRONIC MODEL DESIGN SUPERVISOR · CHRIS BARTON
KEY SCULPTOR · GARY POLLARD
CREATURE MOLD SHOP SUPERVISOR · RAY TRICKER
KEY ANIMATRONIC MODEL DESIGNERS: MONIQUE BROWN, MARK COULIER, MICHELLE TAYLOR
ANIMATRONIC MODEL DESIGNERS: MALCOLM EVANS, JOHN COPPINGER, SHIRLEY COOPER, MARIA BOGGI, KATE MURRAY, TERRY JONES, STEVE WRIGHT, TAMZINE HANKS
ANIMATRONIC MODEL DESIGNERS: JENNY PHELPS, JULIE WRIGHT
KEY ANIMATRONIC MOLD DESIGN: JONATHAN ABBAS-KLAHR
MOLDING TECHNICIAN · MATTHEW SMITH
SCULPTORS: PAUL SPATERI, KATE HILL, HOWARD SWINDELL, SHAUNE HARRISON
CREATURES MOLD FILLER · DARREN ROBINSON
ART FINISHER · ASTRIG AKSERALIAN
SUPERVISING PLASTERER · KEN CLARKE
CHARGEHAND PLASTERER · VAL VASIC
PLASTERER · RAY STAPLES
CREATURES PRODUCTION ASSISTANT · LOUISA RAWLINS
MAKE-UP ARTISTS: MEG SPEIRS, MELISSA LACKERSTEEN
MAKE-UP ARTIST TO LIAM NEESON · MORAG ROSS
MAKE-UP SUPPLIES BY SCREENFACE
WIGS BY WIG SPECIALITIES
CHIEF HAIRDRESSER · SUE LOVE
HAIRDRESSERS: SARAH LOVE, DARLENE FORRESTER
HAIRDRESSER TO LIAM NEESON · JAN ARCHIBALD
ASSISTANT HAIRDRESSER · HELEN TAYLOR
GAFFER · EDDIE KNIGHT
BEST BOY · STEWART MONTEITH
ELECTRICIANS: GARY COLKETT, VERNON CONNOLLY, ADAM LEE, MARK THOMAS, GEORGE WHITE
GENERATOR OPERATORS: TIM WILEY, STUART HURST
ELECTRICAL STOREMAN · COLIN COUGHLIN
RIGGING GAFFER · MARK EVANS
RIGGING ELECTRICIANS: KEITH KIRKUM, LARRY MEEHAN, ROY ROWLANDS, JACK WHITE
ELECTRICAL RIGGERS: SIMON DUTTON, GARRY RIDGEWELL
PRACTICAL ELECTRICIANS: JOHN BARRY, RONALD LYONS, MICKEY O'CONNELL

FIRST ASSISTANT EDITOR · MARYPAT PLOTTNER
AVID ASSISTANT · JOSEPH JETT SALLY
VISUAL EFFECTS EDITORIAL COORDINATOR · PAUL CICHOCKI
FILM ASSISTANT EDITORS: AURA GILGE, DAVID SUTHER
UK ASSISTANT EDITORS: JULIAN PRYCE, JAMIE MARTIN
POST-PRODUCTION ASSISTANT · KERRY BAILEY
COLOR TIMER · JIM PASSON

POST-PRODUCTION SUPERVISORS: MICHAEL BLANCHARD & JAMIE FORESTER

SPECIAL VISUAL EFFECTS AND ANIMATION BY INDUSTRIAL LIGHT & MAGIC, A DIVISION OF LUCAS DIGITAL LTD. LLC, MARIN COUNTY CALIFORNIA

VISUAL EFFECTS EXECUTIVE PRODUCER · CHRISSIE ENGLAND
VISUAL EFFECTS PRODUCERS: NED GORMAN, JEFF OLSON, HEATHER SMITH, GINGER THEISEN, JUDITH WEAVER
DIGITAL MODELING SUPERVISOR · GEOFF CAMPBELL
VIEWPAINT SUPERVISOR · JEAN BOLTE
CREATURE DEVELOPER SUPERVISOR · TIM McLAUGHLIN
LEAD ANIMATORS: LINDA BEL, PETER DAULTON, LOU DELLAROSA, MIGUEL FUERTES, HAL HICKEL, PAUL KAVANAGH, KIM THOMPSON, MARJOLAINE TREMBLAY
VISUAL EFFECTS PRODUCTION DESIGNER · DOUG CHIANG
LEAD COMPUTER GRAPHICS SUPERVISOR · KEVIN RAFFERTY
ASSOCIATE VISUAL EFFECTS SUPERVISOR · BARRY ARMOUR
VISUAL EFFECTS ART DIRECTOR · DAVID NAKABAYASHI
GROUND BATTLE ANIMATION SUPERVISOR · TOM BERTINO
TECHNICAL ANIMATION SUPERVISOR · JAMES TOOLEY
ADDITIONAL VISUAL EFFECTS SUPERVISION · SCOTT FARRAR
COMPUTER GRAPHICS SUPERVISORS: JON ALEXANDER, TIM ALEXANDER, CHRISTOPHE HERY, TOM HUTCHINSON, EUAN MACDONALD, GREG MALONEY, PATRICK T. MYERS, DOUG SMYTHE, HABIB ZARGARPOUR

SEQUENCE SUPERVISORS AND DEVELOPMENT LEADS
KEVIN BARNHILL · SAMIR HOON · STUART MASCHWITZ
STEVE MOLIN · DOUGLAS SUTTON · MICHAEL Di COMO
DORNE HUEBLER · TERRENCE MASSON · HIROMI ONO
CHAD TAYLOR · HOWARD GERSH · MICHAEL LUDLAM
DAVID MENY · AMANDA RONAI-DAHLE · CHRISTOPHER TOWNSEND
DAN GOLDMAN · ROBERT MARINIC · CURT MIYASHIRO
SEAN SCHUR · CHRISTOPHER WHITE

DIGITAL EFFECTS ARTISTS
SHADI ALMASSIZADEH · MICHAEL CONTE · CHRISTINA HILLS
MICHAEL MIN · DOUGLAS J. SMITH · WILL ANIELEWICZ

CAITLIN CONTENT · DAVID HISANAGA · DARYL MUNTON
BRIAN SOBBO · JOAKIM ARNESSON · VINCENT DE QUATTRO
DAVID HORSLEY · JULIE NEARY · CHRISTA STARR
OKAN ATAMAN · DAVID DEUBER · CHRISTOPHER HORVATH
PATRICK NEARY · DAVID STEPHENS · AL BAILEY
JEFF DORAN · PEG HUNTER · KENNETH NIELSEN
CHRIS STILLMAN · MICHAEL BALTAZAR · RUSSELL EARL
POLLY ING · KHATSHO ORFALI · JOHN STILLMAN
ERAN BARNEA · ERIC ENDERTON · ERICH IPPEN
DAVID PARRISH · RUSS SUEYOSHI · MAURICE BASTIAN
JEFF ERTL · SANDRA KARPMAN · EDWARD PASQUARELLO
CATHERINE TATE · KATHLEEN BEELER · GONZALO ESCUDERO
LOUIS KATZ · MARY PAYNE · TIM TERAMOTO
JEFFREY BENEDICT · LEANDRO ESTEBECORENA · STEVE KENNEDY
ELLEN POON · ERIC TEXIER · LEILA BEN-JOSEPH
TOM FEJES · RUSSELL KOONCE · SCOTT PRIOR
MARC TOSCANO · ARON BONAR · DEAN FOSTER
MITCH KOPELMAN · RICARDO RAMOS · ALEX TROPIEC
MATTHEW BOUCHARD · CHRISTIAN FOUCHER · ED KRAMER
PHILIPPE REBOURS · HANS UHLIG · STELLA BOGH
DAVID FUHRER · BRIAN LA FRANCE · KEVIN REUTER
ERIC VOEGELS · GREGORY BRAUER · TODD FULFORD
JEROEN LAPRE · MAX ROCCHETTI · JOHN WALKER
PATRICK BRENNAN · JENNIFER GERMAN · MOHEN LEO
ALAN ROSENFELD · ANDY WANG · BILLY BROOKS
JEREMY GOLDMAN · JOSHUA LEVINE · TOM ROSSETER
ROBERT WEAVER · CATHY BURROW · JOHN K. GOODMAN
LYNDON LI · JONATHAN ROTHBART · SUSAN WEEKS
DON BUTLER · ADRIAN GRAHAM · ALEX LINDSAY
BARRY SAFLEY · DAVID WEITZBERG · MARIO CAPELLARI
MATTHIEU GROSPIRON · CRAIG LYN · FREDERIC SCHMIDT
COLIE WERTZ · TAMALA CARTER · ANDREW HARDAWAY
SIMON MADDOCKS · DURANT SCHOON · KEN WESLEY
IAN CHRISTIE · PABLO HELMAN · TIA MARSHALL
DAN SHUMAKER · MELVA YOUNG · PAUL CHURCHILL
JOHN HELMS · KEVIN MAY · JEFF SHANK
DEAN YURKE · BRIAN CONLON · NEIL HERZINGER
JENNIFER MCKNEW · PAUL SHARPE · KEN ZIEGLER
PATRICK CONRAN · KELA HICKS · KERRY MILLER
LINDA SIEGEL · RITA ZIMMERMAN

CHARACTER ANIMATORS
PHILIP ALEXY · ANDREW DOUCETTE · STEVE LEE
JACQUES MULLER · MAGALI RIGAUDIAS · CHRIS ARMSTRONG
ANDREW GRANT · MARTIN L'HEUREUX · JULIE NELSON
TRISH SCHUTZ · PATRICK BONNEAU · PAUL GRIFFIN
VICTORIA LIVINGSTONE · STEVE NICHOLS · TOM ST. AMAND
SUSAN CAMPBELL · KENT HAMMERSTROM · KEVIN MARTEL
DANA O'CONNOR · GLENN SYLVESTER · MARC CHU
TIM HARRINGTON · GLEN McINTOSH · RICK O'CONNOR
SI TRAN · CHI CHUNG TSE · JASON IVIMEY
NEIL MICHKA · DAVID PARSONS · SCOTT WIRTZ
KYLE CLARK · SHAWN KELLY · CHRISTOPHER MINOS
STEVE RAWLINS · ANDY WONG · BRUCE DAHL
KEN KING · CHRISTOPHER MITCHELL · JAY RENNIE
WILLIAM R. WRIGHT

DIGITAL MODEL DEVELOPMENT AND CONSTRUCTION ARTISTS
STEPHEN APLIN · KEN BRYAN · PAUL GIACOPPO
SUNNY LI-HSIEN WEI · DAVID SACCHERI · DONNA BEARD
ANDREW CAWRSE · DEREK GILLINGHAM · ALYSON MARKELL
TONY SOMMERS · DUGAN BEACH · SIMON CHEUNG
REBECCA HESKES · RUSSELL PAUL · HOWIE WEED
SCOTT BONNENFANT · CATHERINE CRAIG · JEAN-CLAUDE LANGER
AARON PFAU · RON WOODALL · ROBERT BRUCE
AARON FERGUSON · LENNY LEE · COREY ROSEN
ELBERT YEN

DIGITAL MATTE ARTISTS
RONN BROWN · CAROLEEN GREEN · PAUL HUSTON
RICK RISCHE · YUSEI UESUGI · BRIAN FLORA
JONATHAN HARB · BILL MATHER · MARK SULLIVAN
WEI ZHENG

ROTOSCOPE/PAINT SUPERVISORS: SUSAN KELLY-ANDREWS, JACK MONGOVAN
LEAD VISUAL EFFECTS COORDINATOR · LISA TODD
VISUAL EFFECTS PRODUCTION ACCOUNTANT · JOSHUA MARKS
PROJECTIONIST · KENN MOYNIHAN
MOTION CAPTURE SUPERVISOR · JEFF LIGHT
DIGITAL COLOR TIMING SUPERVISORS: BRUCE VECCHITTO, KENNETH SMITH
3D MATCHMOVE SUPERVISORS: KEITH JOHNSON, DAVID WASHBURN
RESEARCH & DEVELOPMENT SUPERVISOR · CHRISTIAN ROUET
ADDITIONAL MATTE PAINTINGS · BILL GEORGE

VISUAL EFFECTS EDITORS: SCOTT BALCEREK, DAVID TANAKA, GREG HYMAN, JOHN BARTLE

VISUAL EFFECTS COORDINATORS
ALEXANDRA ALTROCCHI · MICHAELA CALANCHINI · MONIQUE GOUGEON
AMANDA MONTGOMERY · PENNY RUNGE · LORI ARNOLD
DAVID DRANITZKE · DAVID GRAY · LUKE O'BYRNE
ROBIN SAXEN · LIZ BROWN · VICKI ENGEL
SUSAN GREENHOW · CHRISTINE OWENS · DAVID VALENTIN

DIGITAL ROTOSCOPE/PAINT ARTISTS
TRANG BACH · BETH D'AMATO · SUSAN GOLDSMITH
KATIE MORRIS · ZACHARY SHERMAN · KATHARINE BAIRD
SCOTT DAVID · CAM GRIFFIN · AARON MUSZALSKI
DAVID SULLIVAN · LANCE BAETKEY · KATE ELSEN
JIRI JACKNOWITZ · ANDREW NELSON · JAMES VALENTINE
CHRIS BAYZ · KELLY FISCHER · PATRICK JARVIS
ELSA RODRIGUEZ · MIKE VAN EPS · RENE BINKOWSKI
DAWN GATES · REGAN McGEE · JOE SALAZAR
ERIN WEST

3D MATCHMOVE ARTISTS
ALIA AGHA · DAVID HANKS · DAVID MANOS MORRIS
DANI MORROW · TALMAGE WATSON · JIM HAGEDORN
LUKE LONGIN · JOSEPH METTEN · MELISSA MULLIN
R. D. WEGENER

MOTION-CAPTURE GROUP: ALEXANDRE FRAZAO, DOUGLAS GRIFFIN, ANN McCOLGAN, SETH ROSENTHAL, MICHAEL SANDERS

VISUAL EFFECTS STORYBOARD/CONCEPTUAL ARTISTS: BRICE COX JR., WARREN FU, JULES MANN, NOEL RUBIN

FILM SCANNING AND RECORDING
RANDALL BEAN · MICHAEL CORDOVA · TIM GEIDEMAN
DOUG JONES · JOSH PINES · EARL BEYER
MICHAEL ELLIS · LYDIA GREENFIELD · JAMES LIM
STEPHANIE TAUBERT · ANDREA BIKLIAN · GEORGE GAMBETTA
NANCY JENCKS · TODD MITCHELL · ALAN TRAVIS

VISUAL EFFECTS EDITORIAL STAFF
NIC ANASTASSIOU · EDWIN DUNKLEY · DAWN MARTIN
JIM MILTON · ELLEN SCHADE · CAREY BURENS
NATALEE DJOKOVIC · IAN McCAMEY · MIKE MORGAN
ANTHONY PITONE

SOFTWARE DEVELOPMENT
JOHN ANDERSON · TOMMY BURNETTE · ZORAN KAALESI
NICOLAS POPRAVKA · VINCENT TOSCANO · DAVID BENSON
JOHN HORN · FLORIAN KAINZ · VISHWA RANJAN
ALAN TROMBLA · ROD BOGART · JIM HOURIHAN
CARY PHILLIPS · ERIC SCHAFER · JEFFERY YOST

VISUAL EFFECTS PRODUCTION AND TECHNICAL SUPPORT
NOEL BREVICK · BRIAN GEE · BILL GRINDER
JENNIFER NONA · MARC SADEGHI · SEAN CASEY
KATHY GARDNER · SEAN HOESSLI · MARISA PEARL
LESLIE SAFLEY · MEI MING CASINO · DIANA GAZDIK
JOHN LEVIN · DAVID OWEN · DAMIAN STEEL
FAY DAVID · SAM GRANAT · KIMBERLY LASHBROOK
DON ROTTIERS · BILL TLUSTY · TOM FIRESTONE
KALEEM KARMAN · JONATHAN LITT · MASAYORI OKA
ANTHONY SHAFER · DOUGLAS APPLEWHITE · BRIAN KASPER
DANIEL LOBL · KIM ORLA-BUKOWSKI · MARC WILHITE
CEDRICK CHAN · TODD KRISH · DANA MASINO
MIKE PETERS · CARRIE WOLBERG

DIGITAL OPERATIONS AND TECHNOLOGY GROUP
BRIAN BRECHT · GAIL CURREY · SHANNON HENRY
NANCY LUCKOFF · CLIFF PLUMER · ENDLA BURROWS
VICKI DOBBS BECK · JAY JOHNSON · KEN MARUYAMA
BETH SASSEEN · KIPP ALDRICH · RUSSELL DARLING
MARY HINMAN · RALEIGH MANN · GARY MEYER
KEN BEYER · GREG DUNN · JEFF KING
GARRICK MEEKER · FRED MEYERS · STEWART BIRNAM
SCOTT GRENIER · DAN LEE · WILL MELICK
JOE TAKAI

MINIATURE CONSTRUCTION AND PHOTOGRAPHY UNIT

MODEL SUPERVISOR · STEVE GAWLEY

CHIEF MODEL MAKERS
WILLIAM BECK · BARBARA AFFONSO · BRIAN GERNAND
KEITH LONDON · LORNE PETERSON · STEVE WALTON
CHARLIE BAILEY · GIOVANNI DONOVAN · IRA KEELER
MICHAEL LYNCH

MODEL MAKERS
LAUREN ABRAMS · NICK d'ABO · AARON HAYE

CREDITS

RODNEY MORGAN
FON DAVIS
TREVOR TUTTLE
ERIK JENSEN
SALVATORE BELLECI
RANDY OTTENBERG
MARK FIORENZA
MARK WALAS
VICTORIA LEWIS
NICK BOGLE
TOM PROOST
CHRIS GOEHE
CHUCK WILEY
SCOTT McNAMARA
MARK BUCK
EBEN STROMQUIST

LARRY TAN
GRANT IMAHARA
CAROL BAUMAN
DAVE MURPHY
ROBERT EDWARDS
DANNY WAGNER
KELLY LEPKOWSKI
NICK BLAKE
TONY PRECIADO
JON FOREMAN
KEVIN WALLACE
ALAN LYNCH
PHIL BROTHERTON
MICHAEL STEFFE
PEGGY HRASTAR
ERAN YACHDAV

CARL ASSMUS
WENDY MORTON
BRIAN DEWE
LAUREN VOGT
MICHAEL JOBE
DON BIES
ALAN PETERSON
DAVID FOGLER
MELANIE WALAS
TODD LOOKINLAND
JEFF BREWER
R. KIM SMITH
JON GUIDINGER
JULIE WOODBRIDGE
AMY MILLER

EFFECTS DIRECTORS OF PHOTOGRAPHY: MARTY ROSENBERG, PATRICK SWEENEY, PAT TURNER, RAY GILBERTI
CAMERA OPERATORS: CARL MILLER, VANCE PIPER
ASSISTANT CAMERA OPERATORS: BOB HILL, JOHN GAZDIK, MICHAEL BIENSTOCK
GAFFERS: MICHAEL OLAGUE, TIM MORGAN
KEY GRIPS: BILL BARR, BERNIE DEMOLSKI
CHIEF COSTUMER .... ANNIE POLLAND
CAMERA ENGINEERING: GREG BEAUMONTE, MIKE MACKENZIE, DUNCAN SUTHERLAND
STAGE COORDINATOR .... MEGAN CARLSON

GRIP AND ELECTRIC CREW

JOE ALLEN	RON DIGGORY	DANNY MICHALSKE
CHUCK RAY	DAVE WATSON	TOM CLOUTIER
DENNIS GEHRINGER	CRAIG MOHAGEN	JOHN SILER

SPECIAL EFFECTS .... PYROTECHNICS CREW
SPECIAL EFFECTS SUPERVISOR .... GEOFF HERON
SPECIAL EFFECTS BEST BOY .... ROBBIE CLOT
SPECIAL EFFECTS TECHNICIAN .... DAVE HERON

DATA-CAPTURE SYSTEM SUPPLIED BY ARRI MEDIA, MUNICH
VISUAL EFFECTS PROCESSING & PRINTS BY MONACO LABORATORIES, SAN FRANCISCO
VISUAL EFFECTS CREW FUELED BY MICHAEL SMITH & JAVVA THE HUTT

POST-PRODUCTION SOUND SERVICES PROVIDED BY SKYWALKER SOUND, A DIVISION OF LUCAS DIGITAL LTD. LLC, MARIN COUNTY, CALIFORNIA

RE-RECORDING MIXERS: GARY RYDSTROM, TOM JOHNSON, SHAWN MURPHY
ADR RECORDIST .... MATTHEW WOOD
ADR RECORDED AT COMPASS POINT STUDIOS, NASSAU, BAHAMAS MAGMASTERS
FOLEY MIXER .... TONY ECKERT
FOLEY RECORDIST .... FRANK "PEPE" MEREL
FOLEY ARTISTS: DENNIE THORPE, JANA VANCE
RE-RECORDIST .... RONALD G. ROUMAS
MIX TECHNICIANS: TONY SERENO, JURGEN SCHARPF
SUPERVISING SOUND EDITORS: BEN BURTT, TOM BELLFORT
CO-SUPERVISING SOUND EDITOR .... MATTHEW WOOD
SOUND EFFECTS EDITORS: TERESA ECKTON, CHRIS SCARABOSIO
DIALOGUE/ADR EDITORS: SARA BOLDER, GWENDOLYN YATES WHITTLE
FOLEY EDITORS: BRUCE LACEY, MARIAN WILDE
ASSISTANT SOUND EDITORS: KEVIN SELLERS, STEVE SLANEC
ASSISTANT DIALOGUE/ADR EDITOR .... JESSICA BELLFORT
DIGITAL AUDIO TRANSFER SUPERVISOR ..... JONATHAN GREBER
DIGITAL AUDIO TRANSFER: DEE SELBY, KENT SPARLING
MACHINE ROOM OPERATORS: BRANDON PROCTOR, STEPHEN ROMANKO, JENNIFER BARIN, CHRISTOPHER BARRON
VIDEO SERVICES: CHRISTIAN VON BURKLEO, JOHN TORRIJOS
PROJECTIONIST .... SCOTT BREWER
MUSIC EDITOR .... KEN WANNBERG
ASSISTANT MUSIC EDITOR .... PETER MYLES
ORCHESTRATIONS: JOHN NEUFELD, CONRAD POPE
MUSIC RECORDED AT ABBEY ROAD STUDIOS
SCORING ENGINEER .... SHAWN MURPHY
SCORING ASSISTANTS: JONATHAN ALLEN, ANDREW DUDMAN
MUSIC PREPARATION: DAKOTA MUSIC SERVICE, JO ANN KANE MUSIC SERVICE
MUSIC PERFORMED BY THE LONDON SYMPHONY ORCHESTRA
ORCHESTRA LEADER .... GORDAN NIKOLITCH
CHOIRS: LONDON VOICES, NEW LONDON CHILDREN'S CHOIR
CHORUS DIRECTORS: TERRY EDWARDS, RONALD CORP
DIRECTOR OF PUBLICITY .... LYNNE HALE
UNIT PUBLICIST .... KATE CAMPBELL
CHIEF STILLS PHOTOGRAPHER .... KEITH HAMSHERE
STILLS PHOTOGRAPHERS: GILES KEYTE, JONATHAN FISHER
PHOTOGRAPHY ASSISTANT .... DEREK BOYES
STILLS PROCESSING BY PINEWOOD STUDIOS
DOCUMENTARY CINEMATOGRAPHER .... JONATHAN SHENK

DOCUMENTARY SOUND RECORDISTS: MARK BECKER, GUY HAKE
IMAGE ARCHIVIST .... TINA MILLS
RESEARCHERS: JO DONALDSON, CHERYL EDWARDS, JENNY CRAIK

SECOND UNIT
SECOND UNIT DIRECTOR .... ROGER CHRISTIAN
DIRECTOR OF PHOTOGRAPHY .... GILES NUTTGENS
FIRST ASSISTANT DIRECTOR .... NICK HECKSTALL-SMITH
SECOND ASSISTANT DIRECTOR .... GEORGE WALKER
THIRD ASSISTANT DIRECTOR .... JANET NIELSEN
SCRIPT SUPERVISOR .... LISA VICK
FOCUS PULLER .... STEVEN HALL
CLAPPER LOADERS: EDWARD MEREDYDD JONES, IAN COFFEY
GRIP .... MARK BINNALL
WARDROBE ASSISTANTS: DAY MURCH, JANE PETRIE, NIGEL EGERTON
ART DIRECTOR .... RICKY EYRES
GAFFER .... DAVID SMITH
CHARGEHAND STAND-BY PROPMAN .... PAUL TURNER
STAND-BY PROPMAN .... ROBERT THORNE
STAND-BY CARPENTER .... PAUL NOTT-MACAIRE
STAND-BY RIGGER .... STEVE SANSOM SR.
MAKE-UP ARTIST .... TREFOR PROUD
HAIRDRESSER .... HILARY HAINES
MATCHMOVER .... CATRIN MEREDYDD
VIDEO PLAYBACK .... LUCIEN NUNES VAZ
BEST BOY .... DAVE RIDOUT
ELECTRICIANS: SONNY BURDIS, RICHARD OXLEY

STAND-IN FOR LIAM NEESON .... GAVIN HALE
STAND-IN FOR EWAN McGREGOR .... STEVE RICARD
STAND-IN FOR NATALIE PORTMAN .... JOAN FIELD
STAND-IN FOR JAKE LLOYD .... RAYMOND GRIFFITHS
UTILITY STAND-INS: PAUL KITE, CHRISTIAN SIMPSON

SPECIAL EFFECTS SUPERVISOR .... PETER HUTCHINSON
SENIOR SPECIAL EFFECTS TECHNICIANS: TERRY GLASS, DIGBY BETTISON-MILNER, ANTHONY PHELAN, LES WHEELER, ANDY BUNCE
SPECIAL EFFECTS COORDINATOR .... BRENDA HUTCHINSON
R2-D2 OPERATOR .... JOLYON BAMBRIDGE
SPECIAL EFFECTS TECHNICIANS: JIM CROCKETT, STEPHEN HUTCHINSON, BARRY ANGUS, MARK HOWARD, SEAN McCONVILLE, GRAHAM RIDDELL

TUNISIA SHOOT
PRODUCTION SERVICES PROVIDED BY CTV SERVICES, TUNIS, TUNISIA
PRODUCTION SUPERVISOR .... ABDELAZIZ BEN MLOUKA
UNIT MANAGERS: MEIMOUN MAHBOULI, PHILIPPA DAY
PRODUCTION COORDINATOR .... AMEL BECHARNIA
LOCATION MANAGER .... MOSLAH KRAIEM
TRANSPORT MANAGER .... LASSAAD MEJRI
PRODUCTION ACCOUNTANT .... ABDALLAH BALOUCHE
ART DIRECTOR .... TAIEB JALLOULI
1ST ASSISTANT DIRECTOR .... MOEZ KAMOUN
PROP MASTER/BUYER .... MOHAMED BARGAOUI
GRIP .... HASSEN TEBBI
GAFFER .... LOTFI SIALA
MAKE-UP ASSISTANT .... HAGER BOUHAOUALA
WARDROBE SUPERVISOR .... NAAMA JAZI MEJRI

ITALY SHOOT
PRODUCTION SERVICES PROVIDED BY MESTIERE CINEMA, VENICE, ITALY
PRODUCTION SUPERVISOR .... GUIDO CERASUOLO
UNIT MANAGER .... ENRICO BALLARIN
PRODUCTION COORDINATOR .... LAURA CAPPATO
PRODUCTION ASSISTANT .... NICOLA ROSADA
FIRST ASSISTANT DIRECTOR .... DAVID TURCHI
SECOND ASSISTANT DIRECTOR .... DARIO CIONI
THIRD ASSISTANT DIRECTOR .... ANDREA BONI
LOCATION MANAGER .... FRANCO RAPA
LOCATION ASSISTANT .... UGO CRISCUOLO
ART DIRECTOR .... LIVIA BORGOGNONI
TRANSPORT CAPTAIN .... FABIO MANCINI
ACCOUNTANT .... CARLA ZACCHIA
PAYROLL .... MARILENA LA FERRARA
CASHIER .... CLAUDIA BRAVIN
TRANSPORT CAPTAIN .... PHIL ALLCHIN

UNIT DRIVERS

GEORGE ANDREWS	NIGEL BIRTCHNELL	GARRY CLARK
PETER COLLINS	MARK DAVIES	BRIAN ESTERBROOK
PETER GRAOVAC	JOHN HOLLYWOOD	CHRIS STREETER
STEVE TIMMS		

CATERING BY HOLLYWOOD CATERING SERVICES
CATERING MANAGER .... TIM DE'ATH
ARTISTES' CHEF .... MARK REYNOLDS
CRAFT SERVICE .... SOPHIE MELLOR

SPECIAL THANKS TO:

JIM MORRIS	GLORIA BORDERS	PATRICIA BLAU
STEVE SMITH	SIMON TAY	DANIEL DARK
SALLY BULLOCK	MAXXIOM LIMITED	RUNCO VIDEO
INTERNATIONAL	PARASOUND-HOME THEATER	DON POST
ANNA BIES	FRAMESTORE, LONDON	CHAPEAU ATELIER
GALLERY SOFTWARE	TUNIS AIR	PEOPLE OF TOZEUR,
TATAOUINE & MEDENINE, TUNISIA		TUNISIAN MINISTRY OF THE INTERIOR
ITALIAN MINISTRY OF ART AND CULTURE		SUPERINTENDENT OF THE
HERITAGE OF CASERTA & BENEVENTO		ITALIAN AIR FORCE
TRAINING SCHOOL FOR NON-COMMISSIONED OFFICERS		GOVERNOR AND
CITY OF CASERTA	POLICE & CARABINIERI OF CASERTA	ITALIAN AIR FORCE
- AIRFIELD CAPODICHINO, NAPLES		HERTS FILM LINK
BRITISH MUSICIANS UNION		AZTEC MODELS
ELECTROHOME PROJECTION SYSTEMS		DOREMI LABS, INC
SONY CORPORATION OF AMERICA		

FILMED AT LEAVESDEN STUDIOS, LEAVESDEN, ENGLAND, AND ON LOCATION IN CASERTA, ITALY, AND TOZEUR, TATAOUINE & MEDENINE, TUNISIA

MIXED & RECORDED IN A THX CERTIFIED FACILITY
COLOR BY RANK (DELUXE) FILM LABORATORIES, UK
PRINTS BY DELUXE LABORATORIES
DAILIES TELECINE BY MIDNIGHT TRANSFER, LONDON
EDITED ON AVID FILM COMPOSER SYSTEM
END CREDITS BY PACIFIC TITLE
NEGATIVE CUTTING BY KONA CUTTING
PRODUCTION VEHICLES BY MICKY WEBB TRANSPORT
PRODUCTION SPEAKER SYSTEMS BY M & K SOUND
LOCATION PROJECTION FACILITIES BY DIGITAL PROJECTION
WESCAM CAMERA BY FLYING PICTURES LTD
UNDERWATER TANK BY ACTION UNDERWATER STUDIOS LTD
PRODUCTION SOFTWARE BY COLUMBUS ENTERTAINMENT
SCRIPTS BY SAPEX SCRIPTS
COMMUNICATIONS EQUIPMENT BY WAV/EVEND LTD
PRODUCTION LEGAL SERVICES BY BILLY HINSHELWOOD - MARRIOTT HARRISON
INSURANCE SERVICES BY DAVID HAVARD & AON/ALBERT G RUBEN
EUROPEAN TRAVEL SERVICES BY SUE ROBERTS - THE TRAVEL COMPANY
US TRAVEL SERVICES BY CATHY NILSEN - DIRECT ACCESS
UK SHIPPING SERVICES BY DYNAMIC INTERNATIONAL FREIGHT SERVICES
US SHIPPING SERVICES BY INTERNATIONAL CARGO SERVICES
DE-HISS PROCESSING BY CEDAR DH-1, HHB COMMUNICATIONS INC.
ON-LINE & TELECINE SERVICES BY WESTERN IMAGES, SAN FRANCISCO
ELECTRIC IMAGE 3D SOFTWARE BY PLAY INC.
COMMOTION VISUAL EFFECTS SOFTWARE BY PUFFIN DESIGNS
DIGITAL STORAGE BY HAMMER STORAGE SOLUTIONS
PRE-VISUALIZATION COMPUTERS BY APPLE
ANIMATION SOFTWARE BY SOFTIMAGE
MAYA SOFTWARE BY ALIAS/WAVEFRONT

LIGHTING EQUIPMENT BY AFM LIGHTING LTD, LONDON

ARRIFLEX CAMERA & HAWK ANAMORPHIC LENSES SUPPLIED BY ARRI MEDIA

SHOT ON KODAK MOTION PICTURE FILM

SOUNDTRACK AVAILABLE ON SONY CLASSICAL
READ THE NOVEL FROM DEL REY BOOKS

DOLBY DIGITAL
SONY DYNAMIC DIGITAL SOUND
DTS DIGITAL SOUND IN SELECTED THEATRES
COMPUTERS BY SILICON GRAPHICS

MOTION PICTURE ASSOCIATION OF AMERICA

THE EVENTS, CHARACTERS AND FIRMS DEPICTED IN THIS PHOTOPLAY ARE FICTITIOUS. ANY SIMILARITY TO ACTUAL PERSONS, LIVING OR DEAD, OR TO ACTUAL EVENTS OR FIRMS IS PURELY COINCIDENTAL

OWNERSHIP OF THIS MOTION PICTURE IS PROTECTED BY COPYRIGHT AND OTHER APPLICABLE LAWS, AND ANY UNAUTHORIZED DUPLICATION, DISTRIBUTION OR EXHIBITION OF THIS MOTION PICTURE COULD RESULT IN CRIMINAL PROSECUTION, AS WELL AS CIVIL LIABILITY.

COPYRIGHT © 1999 LUCASFILM LTD. ALL RIGHTS RESERVED

RELEASED BY TWENTIETH CENTURY FOX FILM CORPORATION

QUALITY ASSURANCE SERVICES WERE PROVIDED BY THE THX THEATRE ALIGNMENT PROGRAM

IF YOU EXPERIENCE ANY CONDITIONS THAT DETRACTED FROM THE THEATRICAL PRESESENTATION OF THIS FILM, PLEASE CALL 1-800-PHONE-THX.

"DON'T MAKE ME DESTROY YOU!"

Look familiar? Scenes like this, fighting over the last available issue of _Star Wars Magazine_, can be avoided by taking one simple action...

SUBSCRIBE AND SURVIVE!

Avoid the pain, the frustration, the wear and tear on your lightsabre. Subscribe today and each bi-monthly issue will be delivered direct to your door, no fuss, and at no additional cost. All you need to do is sit back and relax, like a blasé tree goat high in the branches of Endor's forest moon, and enjoy the latest issue of _Star Wars Magazine_ without doing yourself (or any unsuspecting Dark Lord of the Sith) any damage.

UP TO 15% OFF THE COVER PRICE!

To make the experience even more pleasurable, we've come up with a plan to save you some hard-earned crystalline vertex. If you subscribe for two years, you receive a discount of 15% off the cover price – that's a saving of almost £6.00, or subscribe for 6 issues (one year) you will receive a discount of 10%.

OFFER 1:
ONE YEAR – SIX ISSUES £17.00
OFFER 2:
TWO YEARS – 12 ISSUES £33.00

POST YOUR ORDER TO:

You may telephone your credit card order through on 01858 433169, or fill out the form and fax it to 01858 433715. Office hours are 9.00am to 5.00pm Monday to Friday.

To order by post, send the completed form to:
**Star Wars Subscriptions
Subscriptions Dept. SWSM,
Bowden House,
36 Northampton Road,
Market Harborough,
Leics LE16 9HE.**

Photocopies of this form are acceptable.

ORDER FORM

Yes! I wish to subscribe to _Star Wars Magazine_ for (please tick appropriate box):

☐ 1 year (6 issues) £17.00 (£25.00 for Eire)
☐ 2 years (12 issues) £33.00 (£45.00 for Eire)

Please start my subscription with: ☐ Next issue ☐ Issue Number (please specify)

Name _____

Address _____

_____

Postcode _____ Tel. No. _____

I wish to pay by (please tick as appropriate – Do not send cash):

☐ Cheque ☐ Postal order

Credit card (delete as appropriate): Visa/Mastercard/American Express

Card number (13 or 16 digits) ☐☐☐☐☐☐☐☐☐☐☐☐☐☐☐☐

Expiry date

Please make cheques/postal orders payable to **TITAN BOOKS**

Total amount payable: _____

Signature _____ Date _____

☐ Tick here if you do not wish to receive details of any special offers or new products

Code: SWMS 1 2 3 4 5 6 7 8 9 10